1. GREAT NORTHERN LOON

Lynda Roscoe Hartigan; 4/88

Lynda Roscoe Hartigan; 4/88

THE ART OF THE DECOY:

American Bird Carvings

THE ART OF THE DECOY:

American Bird Carvings

by ADELE EARNEST

DRAWINGS   LOU SCHIFFERL

Schiffer Publishing Ltd

Box E, Exton, Pennsylvania 19341

ART OF THE DECOY

Library of Congress catalog card number: 81-51445

ISBN: 0916838587 Soft
ISBN: 0916838625 Hard
New revised edition, 1982

Printed in the United States of America

2. BLACK DUCKS

CONTENTS

3. CANADA GOOSE

FOREWORD

The American wildfowl decoy is here presented as an art form both useful and beautiful. Originally carved and painted by the wildfowl hunters of America to lure the wild birds out of the sky, decoys are explored here, for the first time, as a folk art.

Although the author's emphasis is on the esthetic value of this oldest native American art, she is equally concerned with the how, where, when, and why of the wildfowl lures.

Nearly ten years ago, as a newcomer to folk art and the museum field, I met Adele Earnest. Since then, I have come to rely on her extensive knowledge and artistic judgments. Her qualifications as an authority on folk art are impressive. She has for fifteen years been co-owner of the Stony Point Folk Art Gallery, in Stony Point, New York, the leading source for museums and collectors of American folk sculpture. Over the years, I have observed her tireless research into the background of the folk sculptures she knows and loves. As fine lures became rare and difficult to find, she increased her study of those that were already in existence, seeking them out in whatever part of the country they might be.

Her expanding knowledge led to this book. It reveals the decoy in a new light, through the individual work of known and of anonymous carvers, and offers to all of us the opportunity to discover a new "old" art form, created out of man's need and inquiring spirit.

Most important, perhaps, Mrs. Earnest's book establishes the decoy as a fascinating, unique, and indigenous American folk art.

Mary Black, Director
Museum of Early American Folk Arts
New York City

4. SANDPIPER

AUTHOR'S NOTE

THE FOLLOWING PHOTOGRAPHS have been chosen to highlight the scope and excellence of this folk art and to reflect the spaces of sea and stream where these extraordinary carvings were used. The text fills in the background, describing the men, the times, and the techniques, insofar as these elements illumine and shape the decoys.

Because space is limited, and because a number of fine decoys proved to be nonphotogenic, not every outstanding example of the wildfowl decoy has been shown or described. I have tried to choose work that is esthetically and historically significant; but I realize the exclusions may seem unfair to carvings of real achievement. Value judgments are so often subjective.

For assistance in assembling the material I would like to thank the many photographers, collectors, museums, and editors who have been most generous with their help.

I am especially indebted to the following gentlemen for allowing me to draw liberally from their knowledge: Paul Wheelock Bigelow, Bellport, New York; Donald Clark, Henry, Illinois; Harold Evans, Watertown, New York; Malcolm J. Fleming, Bellport, New York; Joseph B. French, Clayton, Missouri; Kingdon Hemming (now deceased), Little Silver, New Jersey; Lloyd Johnson, Bay Head, New Jersey; William J. Mackey, Jr., Belford, New Jersey; Thomas C. Marshall, Southport, Connecticut; Hal Sorenson, Burlington, Iowa; George Ross Starr, Duxbury, Massachusetts; Anthony A. Waring, South Swansea, Massachusetts; and Winsor White, Duxbury, Massachusetts.

I am also grateful to Cordelia Hamilton for her encouragement while sharing many long trips with me, and to Robert Eichler for weathering rain and cold on photographic missions.

And finally, I wish to thank Basil Beyea, without whose patient editing this work could not have been possible.

DISCOVERY

5. YELLOWLEGS FOUND ON CAPE COD DUNES

DISCOVERY

It was October, time for the wildfowl to be in full flight over the Barnstable dunes. I had left home early, hoping to see a few black ducks wheel in against the sunset sky as they sought a night's refuge in the quiet marshes of Cape Cod.

Between the dunes and the flat wetland there was a single-track road where only a beach buggy could navigate easily. I parked my car and went my way on foot.

Not another human being was in sight. It was too early for hunters and too late for tourists. There was no sound except the rustle of the sedge grass and the distant boom of the sea breaking on the outer beach. I was the only interloper.

But there were no ducks. Not a wing graced the sky. The whole far reach of estuary was empty. Even my field glasses failed to pick up any movement, any hint of that infinitesimal curl on the horizon that grows steadily into a flock of wild duck coming across the bay. There was nothing, not even a hopeful speck. A few desultory herring gulls dipped by, coasting the airways.

But it was a perfect day to be near the sea. Happily, the times of the birds are the best of the year. When the birds come north in the spring the ground is still damp and cold, but the breeze is gentle on the cheek. In the fall, when they return, the summer colors have deepened, turning the sedge grasses into plum, russet, and gold under the incredible blue of the sky.

Heading back to my car, disappointed but content to be part of a most satisfactory world, I caught sight of a small bird glistening on a sand hummock. It didn't move. I didn't move. I walked nearer. My shadow fell across the figure before I realized it was a wooden rather than a real bird. Its color was bleached like an old bone by the sun and wind. When I picked it up, a leg crumpled in my hand. But it was still a beauty, stout of body.

Later, I learned it was a wildfowl decoy, a yellowlegs, left and forgotten by some wildfowler long ago.

I had never known that the early baymen and woodsmen living along our waterways had carved these magical birds. Magical they were, because their quiet presence on a sandy beach or floating on a pond could attract and beguile the wildfowl out of the sky, within range of man's weapon, and into man's cooking pot. Cape Cod, which lies directly in the path of the great Atlantic flyway, was one of the first lands to welcome the white settlers from Europe. Food in this new country was plentiful but not easy to come by. The unspoiled marshes, rivers, and pine forests teemed with birds, fish, wild turkey, and deer, but everything was on the hoof or on the wing, not packaged at the corner store.

The fish had to be hooked. The succulent goose and the fat mallard duck had to be lured, outwitted, and bagged. And the hunter had to summon all his wits, skills, and arts to do it. Baked, crusty plover pie or roast duck was sweet to eat after a diet of salt pork, dried corn, and beans.

Millions of ducks, geese, curlew, and plover crossed the open skies during the migration season. But birds fly high. The problem was how to bring this quarry down to earth.

One answer was the decoy. The Indians had learned, and the new Americans were quick to learn, that wood, rushes, or any handy material worked into the shapes of birds and set provocatively along the shore or in the water could lure these birds of passage. The art developed out of the necessity.

Since that first discovery of the yellowlegs—my first inkling of the existence of such carvings—I have pursued these attractive arts with a steadily growing delight.

Fifteen years ago the good examples were not too hard to find. There was that auction in Orleans, Massachusetts. In the top drawer of an antique schoolmaster's desk I discovered, wrapped in a linen handkerchief, a tiny sanderling decoy with an N scribed under the tail, and there was also an embroidered N on the kerchief. It looked like a keepsake of some sort.

A Captain Newcombe had lived in the house until 1901. And the Captain had made many decoys. But his energetic grandson had cleaned out the boatshed before the sale, had dumped baskets of the old birds down a woodchuck hole to fill it, and finally had driven his truck back and forth over the hole "to pack them down good."

In North Carolina, a gunny sack of old curlews turned up unexpectedly. The curlew decoy, one of the rarest, is large as shorebirds go, with a full, curvaceous body accented by the dramatic thrust of a long, probing bill.

I had stopped my car at a "Shrimp for Sale" sign near Currituck. On the back seat rested my own lures—a new set of ruddy duck decoys.

The storekeeper 'lowed as he was an old game hunter himself and toted out his old curlew decoys to prove it. We traded bird for bird. He was so pleased he could hardly stand it. After all, he did get a brand-new set of working, store-bright duck decoys in exchange for eighteen old, weathered, handmade curlews that no one could shoot over. Hunting the curlew has been illegal for years. It never occurred to him that I wanted the handsome, antique carvings for their own sake.

It was in Woodstock, New York—far from shore, lake, or estuary—that I found as fine a pair of heron decoys as I have ever seen. I had had little thought of searching for decoys in that landlocked, mountainous terrain, but every time I drove by a certain flagpole I noticed a pigeon sitting on it, and it was always the same one. When I eventually awoke to the fact that the bird was a carving, I was out of the car at once, knocking at the door.

6.   BLUE HERON

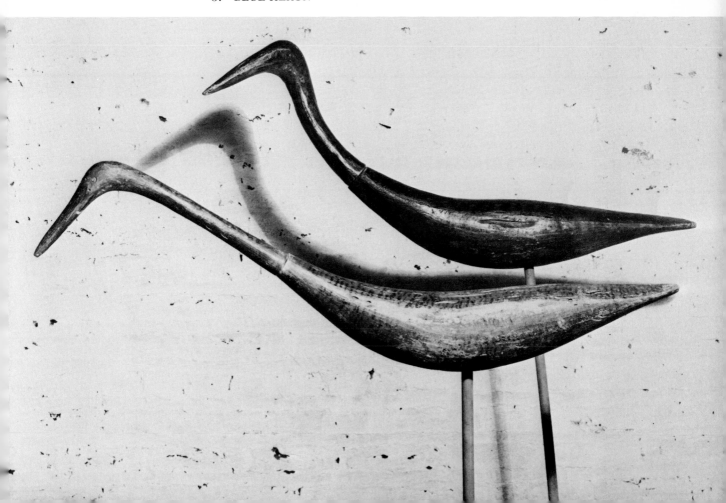

A charming gentleman in a green corduroy suit greeted me, said the pigeon was his, made by him, not a decoy, and not for sale. But he did have a couple of "old birds."

I followed him to his studio and found a hodgepodge of half-finished canvases, frames, paint cans, and still-life props. But in the corner stood a pair of antique heron decoys that took my breath away.

In later years, Stuart Preston, art critic of *The New York Times,* saw them and reported they were "worthy of Brancusi." Today, these superb examples of the art of the American decoy are proudly displayed at The Rochester Memorial Art Museum.

Who was this American "Brancusi"? No one knows. Most decoys are anonymous. Folk art, by its very nature, is the work of people, not of names. Some unknown, unschooled hunter, with no thought of "art" or the here-after, had made these heron for use, as a tool; but fortunately, he had also expressed his own feeling for nature, and his desire to make something beautiful as well as practical.

It is sad that the decoy, as a folk expression, is being recognized so late. Many pieces that should have been treasured have been lost or destroyed—and recently.

The one completely original swan decoy I possess was actually snatched from a bonfire. That was in Maryland, where the wide Chesapeake, rich with tempting wild celery and aquatic plants, attracts the most populous migration stream of wildfowl in the East.

7. SWAN

The day was bright and sunny—a March day with that quickening air of spring. All the roads were clear of ice, and the brooks and farm ponds were overflowing and greening at the edge.

As I was driving leisurely along a detour, I suddenly saw an enormous fire beside the road. It proved to be no more than a controlled bonfire, which crackled and sputtered by an old barn; near it, a farmer was methodically walking back and forth, cleaning out the clutter and feeding the blaze.

8. SHOREBIRD DECOYS WAITING FOR THE HUNTER

I got out to look around. Old barns have a way of producing beaten-up treasures: an early rooster weathervane, blown down in some northeaster; or a ship's lantern; or even a snipe decoy, lying in dust on the rafters.

As I walked closer, I saw that the blaze was a flaming pyre of swan decoys. I shrieked like a Valkyrie—and behaved like one. I rushed at the fire, seized one swan by its long white neck, threw it to the ground, and beat out the flames. The farmer stood transfixed. Breathlessly, I tried to explain—but could not. Finally, he did accept—and gingerly—the five-dollar bill I offered. I did not have the heart to tell him that he had burned up a pile of swan decoys worth at least a thousand dollars.

THE STORY OF THE DECOY

Decoy Carver in Workshop

THE STORY OF THE DECOY

THE AMERICAN SCENE

WHY DID THE DECOY ARTS develop only in America? Wildfowling has been practiced by most civilizations since man started to hunt and make weapons, lures, and talismans in an effort to control nature, find food, and live. But on other continents, and at other times, other methods of catching birds dominated.

Although a scattering of old decoys is to be found in Europe, their use was not general and probably derived from contact with the American scene. The only mention of ancient decoys is in a brief report of hunting arts practiced in Greece. But no remains of such decoys have ever been found in Europe, the Middle East, or the Far East.

It is evident that only in North America, because of a unique combination of circumstances, did the carving of wildfowl lures develop as a popular art of diverse and multitudinous proportions.

The first happy contribution to this propitious state of affairs was provided by the birds themselves. They were here. Up and down this continent flew the largest bird migrations in the world. A flight of geese could take all day to pass, and then darken the face of the moon by night. The wildfowler had rich opportunities.

The next contributing factor was necessity. The new settlers needed game to augment their food supplies. In the 1630's, an unexpected but timely flight of snow geese helped to save the Plymouth Colony in Massachusetts. Enough geese were captured, shot, and bagged to feast upon and to salt down against the harsh, cold winter months.

A third factor favoring the growth of the decoy arts was the freedom of this new land. A man could walk anywhere. He could hunt and fish and boat all along the vast coastal beaches and inland waterways. Down the valley of the Mississippi, golden prairies rolled without fence or wire or sign for a thousand miles. The Great Lakes in the North held half the fresh water in the world. America was a land of endless horizons.

MIGRATION ROUTE
OF THE
GOLDEN PLOVER

In the nineteenth century, hunting guns of superior efficiency made their appearance. The Kentucky rifle, which originated in Pennsylvania, was a remarkable improvement over the old matchlock, wheel lock, and flintlock. Its range was a good hundred yards. No previous gun could have hit an elephant at that distance.

Another weapon that became especially popular with wildfowl hunters because of its lightness, speed, and accuracy was the twelve-gauge shotgun. It is still commonly used by our wildfowlers.

But none of these favorable elements would have produced the arts of the decoy if the basic notion had not already been here: the idea of making a bird to catch a bird. Long before the coming of the white man, the American Indian had conceived this brilliant notion. There is archaeological proof that the Indians made decoys at least as early as A.D. 1000.

WILDFOWL MIGRATIONS

The prime reason for the early emergence of the decoy arts was naturally the wildfowl migration itself, the seemingly miraculous appearance of millions of feathered creatures heading north every spring and reappearing every fall.

Toward the end of March, or early in April, according to the weather, the birds came, nature's chemistry driving them to pick up from their comfortable southern quarters and fly north to Canada and the far reaches of the Arctic, where they had been born and where their young would be born to continue the cycle.

In this northernmost breeding ground, space and privacy for wooing and nesting were practically unlimited, and food was plentiful. The hot, concentrated northern summer produced a superabundance of berries, fat bugs, and lemmings.

When the babies were grown and strong enough to fly, and as the arctic sun paled and began to sink into the dark of the winter night, they left. The various breeds gathered together for days, as if summoned to an avian convocation. Then, at a given signal from one of the elders, they were off.

Ducks, geese, snipe, curlew—all flew back in their highly organized groups, led by seasoned pilots, along charted skyways, across continents and across oceans, thousands of miles back to the warmth of Central and South America.

The tide of their coming and going was as regular as the season itself. And every hunter worth his salt knew the timetable and the route. When the first pintail was sighted off Barnegat Light, or a yellowlegs at Nauset Marsh, the word traveled along the coast that the birds were on the move. The news always meant the expectation of a feast; the spring flight heralded the end of winter and the opening of roads, doors, and communication.

When the time came, the wildfowler shouldered his gun and bag of decoys, and headed for the beaches. There he would set his rig, his wooden ducks or snipe, and then hide, just like an Indian. If he was lucky, he would see his quarry sweep in out of the blue, falter at the sight of his lures—and there would be roast duck on his whirly spit that night.

Through the centuries, up and down this continent, four main routes of travel had been established and followed more or less consistently: the Atlantic, the Mississippi, the Plains, and the Pacific flyways.

Christopher Columbus, approaching the New World, noted in his diary on October 9, 1492: "All night we heard birds passing." The *Santa Maria* was crossing under the Atlantic flyway.

The number of birds that passed over any flyway was incalculable. In Minnesota, the wood ducks came like rain in the tropics, pouring into every pool until the woodlands were deluged.

The Indians could not understand where the birds went when they disappeared. One legend said they flew to the moon. Another told how they hid in caves or trees until their second coming. Today, we have a pretty good idea where they go, but we are far from understanding the biological process that drives them or the built-in radar system that guides them over the trackless miles. The latest belief is that a bird's ear canal is, like a compass, sensitive to terrestrial magnetism.

The three-thousand-mile flight of the golden plover from the Arctic to Patagonia is an unbelievable feat. Today, one speaks of the goldens' spectacular flight in the past tense: though they are not extinct, their numbers have been greatly reduced. Their route took them from Nova Scotia over open ocean toward Bermuda, and thence over open seas again to Venezuela, and from the Orinoco to the Argentine. In stormy weather, the winds drove their flight inland over Cape Cod and Nantucket Island, the only area where golden plover decoys may be found.

The goldens' flight back in the spring was more landbound and more hazardous. On their return from Patagonia, the plover scaled the Andes Mountains of Peru, then followed the Pacific to Honduras, where they crossed the Gulf of Mexico and entered the Mississippi flyway.

John J. Audubon reported seeing "hundreds of thousands" of golden plover over the Louisiana marshes. In fact, there were so many that the hunter did not have to use decoys. On March 11, 1821, while visiting in New Orleans, Audubon wrote in his rough, earthy manner:

I took a Walk with my Gun this afternoon to see the Passage of Millions of *Golden Plovers*. . . . [The] Sportsmen are here more numerous and at the same time more expert at shooting on the Wing than any where in the U. Stantes. On the first sight of these birds Early this Morning [they] assembled in Parties of from 20 to 100 at Diferent places where they Knew by experience they told

Snipe Hunter

me the birds pass and arranged themselves at equal distances squatted on their hams; as a flock Came Near every man Called in a Masterly astonishing Manner, the Birds Imediately Lowered and Wheeled and coming about 40 or 50 yards [ran] the Gantlet. Every Gun goes off in Rotation, and so well aimed that I saw several times a flock of 100 or More Plovers destroyed at the exception of 5 or 6 . . . —from the firing before & behind us I would suppose that 400 Gunners were out. Supposing each Man to have Killed 30 Dozen that day 144,000 must have been destroyed—[1]

Much later in the century, the ornithologist Herbert R. Job reported:

The last really great flight of both these species [golden plover and Eskimo curlew] which I witnessed was in late August, 1883, at Chatham, Mass., at the southern end of the projection of Cape Cod. The wind was shrieking, and I hardly could stand against it on the exposed headlands, where I watched great compact masses of these wonderful birds, high in air, blowing in from the sea.[2]

Unhappily, gunning has rarely changed transcontinental flight patterns, as do fluctuating air currents or a loss of feeding and nesting grounds. The passenger pigeon, which once made up about one-third of our entire bird population, is now extinct in North America: their flight pattern followed the same course year after year, and they were slaughtered mercilessly and unrelentingly. After one day's hunting, a man could drive home a "horse-load" of wild pigeons. The last passenger pigeon died in 1914 at Cincinnati's Zoological Park.

People are often repelled by the realization that decoys were made essentially for the killing of birds. But with the exception of the market gunner, it should be noted that the hunter and the naturalist were often the same person. Audubon traveled with gun as well as paper and pencil.

Hunting has been a springboard for the arts from the time of the cave man and his animistic drawings. Many highly revered Oceanic and African arts consist basically of hunting equipment—often stained with the blood of men rather than birds.

Polynesia war clubs, Kenya shields, and Eskimo fishing spears did not have to be artfully wrought in order to work, and neither did the decoy. Hunters know that almost any old "block" will bring in the wildfowl, if they are feeling curious.

The wooden decoy appeals to us today, not simply because it was a hunting device, but because in the making, in the carving and the painting, the hunters satisfied their natural need for expression, their need to create. And so, a folk art was born.

INDIAN LURES: THE FIRST DECOYS

The first known American decoys date from about A.D. 1000. Archaeologists from the Heye Foundation of the Museum of the American Indian in New York City excavated eleven duck decoys while digging for Indian relics

9. BASKET OF INDIAN DECOYS

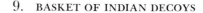

in Lovelock Cave, Nevada, in 1924. It was an exciting moment when the decoys in their basket wrappings were brought out into the light of day; the discovery was considered one of the most important of the entire "dig."

Two kinds of decoys were found in the cave: the canvasbacks, formed out of native bulrushes that had been woven, twisted, and tied into birdlike shapes; and others of uncertain species, made by mounting stuffed skins and the heads of actual birds into lifelike poses.

Whether the cave had been used as living quarters or as a storage pit is unknown. Or, to quote the expedition's report, perhaps "some wildfowl hunter had hidden his decoys against another season."

Several of these ancestors of our present decoys were in almost mint

10. CANVASBACK DECOY

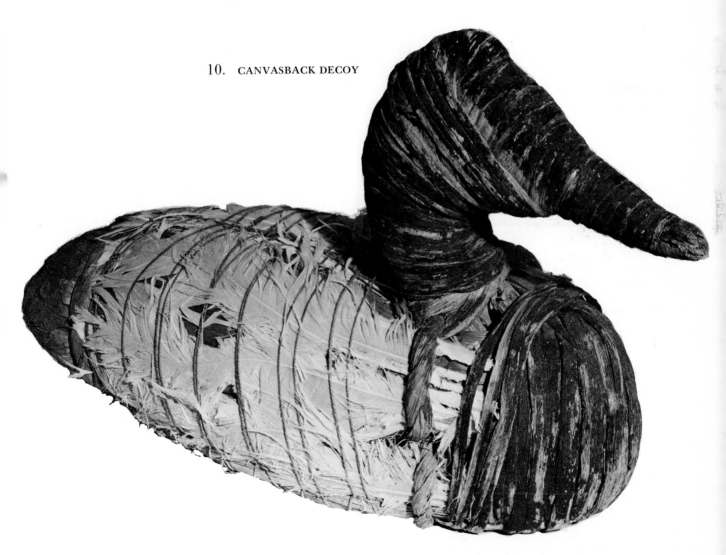

11. PASSERINE DECOY

condition. The canvasback is immediately recognizable by the broad white saddle of feathers bound to its body, the unmistakable wedge-shaped head, and the red sienna of its head and neck.

A number of these prehistoric canvasback decoys, as well as those of some smaller birds, may be seen at the Museum of the American Indian. One decoy, probably a passerine, is under five inches. The frontal part of the head is the skeleton of a real bird. Rushes, wrapped by a pliant twig, make the stuffing over which a natural bird skin, with the feathers, was stretched.

Here is an excerpt from the archaeological report of the discovery:

The decoys found in the Lovelock cave fall into two types, the painted and the stuffed. In the former the body was formed by bending a bundle of 25 or 30 large bulrush (tule) stems (*Scirpus validus*) and binding them together. . . . The ends were then cut off to simulate the duck's tail, and a head was cleverly constructed of rushes and smoothly bound with the same material split, then sewed fast to the body, with evident care to attain a realistic pose. . . . To complete the decoy it was then only necessary to paint the head, breast, and tail to represent the bird, using black and reddish-brown native paints, and to cover the body with white feathers, the quills of which were stuck under the breast-wrappings, and held fast elsewhere with fine native cord of Indian hemp (*Apocynum cannabinum* L.). . . .

Only ducks seem to have been represented by these painted decoys; but ducks, geese, and other water fowl were imitated by the stuffed type, which was commoner, easier to make, and is still manufactured by the Northern Paiute. The body of the stuffed type was made in approximately the same way as the painted type, but the breast was not bound, and instead of a rush head, a sort of rush stub or nipple projected from the body to which a complete stuffed head of the bird was fastened, with its natural skin, feathers, and beak. Sometimes there was enough body skin attached to the head to cover the rush body, but usually it had to be more or less supplemented by small bunches of feathers, the quills of which were stuck into the rushes. . . . Some of the ancient decoys still show a loop of cord on the breast for the attachment of an anchor, and one had a short string under the tail, the loose end tied to the middle of a bit of quill, which doubtless served as a toggle for the attachment of an anchor cord on this end also.[3]

The last sentence, mentioning bits of cord on the ancient duck decoys, indicates that the Indians used floating lures, as we do today.

Another part of the report speaks of the small birds as "mounted." This could mean that the birds were set on sticks, like our shorebird "stickups," rather than mounted in the taxidermist's sense.

12.   CONTEMPORARY PAIUTE INDIAN DECOY: CANVASBACK HEN

13. BOTTOM VIEW OF PAIUTE DECOY: TULE RUSH

The ducks made today by the Northern Paiute Indians show a striking similarity to the old decoys in materials used and type of construction. At the museum there is a contemporary hen canvasback made of rushes and cloaked with a bird skin in fine feather. The decoy is fourteen and a half inches long, the standard length.

Bird skins and feathers propped on some sort of frame continued in popular use with Eastern white hunters up into the twentieth century. Decoys made for this treatment were called "bird-skins," and many were handsome and meticulously formed.

Gideon Lippincott, of Wading River, New Jersey, made just such a fine black duck of bent wood and canvas about 1870. The nails for fastening the skin can be seen at the base of the decoy. The fragility of the feathers and the care required for handling must have made this practice rather impractical. (Incidentally, the nails in the yellowlegs decoy found on the dunes of Cape Cod are evidence that feathers were also used on shorebird decoys.)

Another interesting item in the Lovelock Cave report is the listing of bird skeletons retrieved at the site. Bones from the following birds were dusted off, expertised, and tagged: merganser, sprig, white-fronted goose, ring-necked duck, Canada goose, and pelican. Evidently, a variety of colorful birds enlivened the skies of Nevada a thousand years ago.

14. BLACK DUCK BIRD-SKIN DECOY

How these original Americans, these Indians, captured their game after the decoys did their job of luring the fowl to earth is anyone's guess. They may or may not have shot them with bow and arrow. The throwing stick was popular among the Indians, as with most primitive people.

John J. Audubon, during his travels up and down America in the 1840's, wrote of receiving a present of six young mallard ducks an Indian squaw had caught by swimming after them in the Missouri River and grabbing them by their feet!

No one knows, of course, how it happened that an Indian first got the idea of making an artificial bird to catch a live one. I can imagine that it came about something like this: An Indian brave, relaxing in the spring sun and enjoying the warmth on his bare back, watched the canvasbacks flying overhead. He listened to their pleasant gabble as they rode the light wind in spider-like formation, wave after wave of them as far as he could see. With his hands he idly began to shape the marsh mud and rushes into pleasant forms—birds of his own fancy, but like the heavenly couriers above. He set them out in a row before him and dozed. And then, suddenly, it happened. A duck broke from its flock, swung over the marsh, and pitched down before him.

Was it a miracle? What lured this wild bird from the sky? What hidden power? What magic? Could man with his own handiwork—this pile of mud and straw and sticks—catch the bird-spirit in a manmade image?

Today, we call this magic—"art."

Canada Geese Migrating in Storm

EARLY RECORDS

There is little written record in old diaries, letters, or journals on the use of the decoy by the Indians and the early settlers. In fact, information on all hunting and fishing methods in America during the eighteenth and early nineteenth centuries is sparse.

The earliest account is contained in *New Voyages to North-America* by Baron Lahontan (1666–1715), who was Lord Lieutenant of the French Colony in Newfoundland. His letters contain "an account of the Customs, Commerce, Religion and Strange Opinions of the Savages of that Country." In a letter dated May 28, 1687, he described a hunting trip with the Indians in the marshes of the Missisquoi Delta of northern Lake Champlain:

> In the beginning of September, I set out in a Canow upon several Rivers, Marshes, and Pools that disembogue in the Champlain Lake, being accompany'd with thirty or forty of the Savages that are very expert in Shooting and Hunting and perfectly well equipped with the propper places for finding Water foul, Deer, and other fallow Beasts. The first Post we took up was upon the side of a Marsh or Fen of four or five Leagues in Circumference; and after we had fitted up our Hutts, the Savages made Hutts upon the Water in several places. These Water-Hutts are made of the branches and leaves of Trees, and contain three or four Men. For a Decoy they have the skins of Geese, Bustards, and Ducks, dry'd and stuff'd with Hay. The two feet being made fast with two Nails to a small piece of a light plank, which floats around the Hutt. This place being frequented by wonderfull numbers of Geese,

Ducks, Bustards, Teals, and an infinity of other Foul unknown to the Europeans; when these Fouls see the stuff'd Skins swimming with the Heads erected, as if they were alive, they repair to the same place, and so give the Savages an opportunity of shooting 'em, either flying, or upon the Water; after which the Savages get into their Canows and gather 'em up.[4]

Wildfowl were evidently not common fare for the redmen, but a special treat, because Lahontan later wrote: "When they killed Partridge, a Goose, or a Duck . . . they never failed to present it to their oldest Relations."

"Turtle-Doves," however, were exceptionally numerous. Lahontan told how they so filled the trees during the eighteen or twenty days of their migration that a thousand men might have eaten of them heartily.

Alexander Wilson, who, between 1808 and 1814, wrote the first American ornithology, describes decoy practices in some detail:

The Geese which he [an Indian] has killed, he sets upon sticks, as if alive, to decoy others; he also makes artificial birds for the same purpose. In a good day, for they fly in very uncertain and unequal numbers, a single Indian will kill two hundred.

On hunting for the mallard duck, Wilson is even more explicit:

In some ponds frequented by these birds, five or six wooden figures are painted so as to represent ducks, and sunk by pieces of lead nailed to their bottoms, so as to float at the usual depth on the surface. . . .[5]

Robert Cantwell, a biographer of Wilson's, describes how Wilson went duck hunting with friends:

When people speak of wild ducks they generally meant the mallard. They were already so shy in 1796 that they were hunted with difficulty, usually from skiffs hidden in the reeds or from hogsheads buried in the sand on the shore, with carved decoys anchored a few yards away. But in the Delaware, frames holding as many as ten decoys were sometimes fastened around a skiff, the skiff covered with reeds, and the whole set adrift with the current. When the first cakes of ice appeared in the river, it was possible to approach a flock of mallards if a hunter concealed himself in a skiff painted white and floated within gunshot with the floating ice.[6]

In 1844, Jacob Giraud wrote vividly about hunting the Canada goose on Long Island:

> . . . he [the hunter] has watched their flight and discovered their favorite sanding place; the long neglected decoys are placed in his skiff, and before daylight has appeared, he is pulling his way across the rough bay with glorious anticipation of profit. On gaining the desired point, he puts out his decoys, sinks a box in the sand, and there lies concealed. As they approach, his keen eye glances quickly over his trusty gun, and ere a moment elapses, death is among them. . . .[7]

During the latter half of the nineteenth century, many manuals and sporting publications contained anecdotes about the popular use of the decoy.

THE MARKET GUNNER AND CONSERVATION

Our story has its black pages. In the late nineteenth century the market gunner appeared and initiated a wholesale slaughter of our wildlife. He killed not for his own use, but to sell at market. Barrels of curlew, doves, plover, ducks, and even robins were shipped to the party-givers of the big cities. Two men with a double-barreled shotgun could bag six hundred birds in a day. In Minneapolis, teal sold for ten cents apiece, and a canvasback could fetch as much as fifty cents.

In the years following the Civil War, recovery and industrial expansion led inevitably to exploitation of our resources. We opened up the West, sent our railroads across plain and mountain, and amassed the gigantic oil and coal monopolies. In the process, we also plundered our forests and our soil, decimated our wildlife, and drove the Indian from his native land. The decoy, which had started out as a brilliant way of inducing nature to serve man, went full circle and nearly succeeded in destroying the goal it sought.

To supply the market gunner, whose rig often included a hundred and fifty "coys," manufacturing companies began to sell decoys made of wood, tin, and iron—especially in the Middle West. These companies were small, employing only a few men, but by the 1890's their output was large enough and their product cheap enough to discourage the making of decoys at home.

Fortunately, the old art of making decoys did survive, for many rural hunters preferred their own tollers to the factory products, and some could not afford the purchase price of the "store-bought" decoy.

In fact, after conservation measures prohibited the sale of wildfowl and

Silhouette Decoys

The Market Gunner

37

outlawed battery shooting, the manufacturing companies closed shop, and there was a revival of the old arts. Gunners started to make their own decoys again and to rescue and save the fine old examples of this hunting art.

In 1913, a federal migratory bird act prohibited all spring shooting, all night shooting, and the shipment of birds. In 1918, the Migratory Bird Treaty Act, which we entered into with Canada, protected the waterfowl of North America over the entire range of its migratory flight, and brought an end to all shorebird gunning with the exception of the Wilson snipe, which does not come to the decoy.

And so, finally, overgunning, unlimited take, market gunning, spring shooting, sale of gamebirds, and use of live birds as decoys were outlawed. Today, each state has its own restrictions as to season length, bag limit, and shooting hours—and hunting licenses are required.

In defense of the hunter, it should be noted that most of the conservation measures for preserving wildlife, forest cover, marsh lands, and clean water have been promoted by organizations of hunters and sportsmen as well as by conservationists. The life of our wildfowl in these times is less threatened by the gun than by change of land use, the shrinkage of wintering and feeding areas, and pollution.

Great wildfowl sanctuaries in the West like Horseshoe Lake, Bear Run, and the Salton Sea protect our wildfowl and allow them to multiply. In the East, there are three large federal refuges: Brigantine National Wildlife Refuge, Bombay Hook, and Blackwater. In all, the federal government is sponsoring about three hundred protected areas of swamp, marsh, and wetlands along the four major flyways.

We are finally making a concerted effort to re-establish and cherish the wildfowl that provided so hospitably for our forefathers when, hungry and empty-handed, they came to these shores.

A FOLK ART UNIQUE IN HISTORY

Most of our early arts and crafts were not indigenous. They were either brought here from Europe or were based on European traditions. Once here, these imported skills and styles were quickly adapted to local use, especially in the years following the Revolution, when this new, young nation developed an intensely patriotic and regional feeling.

For example, those ship figureheads that had flaunted the English lion or royal persons were scuttled. In their place, riding the bows of our frigates and clippers, were Washington, Jefferson, Jackson, and sometimes—Pocahontas.

Similarly, the weathervanes designed after the family pennant were scrapped for images taken from the local scene: The Indian, the whale, and the deer marked the spirit of the times as well as the direction of the wind. The fierce Hapsburg eagle acquired an almost friendly look when his visage was redesigned to appear on our courthouses and customs buildings as the symbol of the new republic.

But the modest decoy did not have to experience this Americanization. *It* was here. Europe, in fact, learned about decoys from us—a novel switch in cultural relations. Although a few old decoys have been found abroad, especially in England and in Italy, they probably resulted from contact with America. All evidence points to the fact that the decoy did not develop as a hunting art in Europe, if only because there was no need for it. Other fowling methods had long been established and were continuously popular. The Saxons had set the pattern in England. First, they would build an enclosure of wattles. Then, by beating drums and blowing trumpets, they would drive the bewildered birds into their trap, where they were killed.

In time, this Saxon custom became elaborated into a very English maze of landscaped ponds, funnels, nets, traps, and cages. It was not until the middle of the nineteenth century that this technique was simplified. It was ultimately discarded in favor of live decoys, "stool pigeons," and professional "callers." Trained men were hired to imitate the bird calls and to whistle down the unsuspecting quarry to within comfortable shooting range of the gentry. This type of wildfowling is rightly called duck shooting, instead of duck hunting.

For the commoner, the opportunity to hunt was limited. Lands were restricted, and poaching was severely punished. The weather itself curbed his enthusiasm, inasmuch as the migrating fowl passed over the continent late in the fall, when the season was apt to be inclement and rough.

There is no tangible evidence that the decoy arts developed either in Europe or in any land other than America. I have searched for some kind of artifact, picture, or rendering in other cultures, East and West, but I have found nothing that even suggests the popular use of the decoy anywhere else in the world.

The murals in Egyptian tombs are alive with birds. This is not surprising, since the slow, gliding length of the Nile and its wide, hospitable delta must have been a bird's paradise. But the figures represent live birds, not decoys.

Hunting methods are frequently depicted. For example, a wall painting from the Tomb of Menena at Thebes, Eighteenth Dynasty, *c.* 1415 B.C.,

15. EGYPTIAN FISHING AND FOWLING SCENE

16. EGYPTIAN FOWLING SCENE

shows a dark-skinned fowler in elegant robes in the act of catching ducks by hand and using a kind of throwing stick or boomerang. The whole scene is ritualistic as well as representational. The marsh, teeming with fish and fowl, represents the "lake of life" through which the fowler voyages to another world. The wild duck stands for the evil to be exterminated as well as game to be tracked down.

A scene from the Tomb of Khum-hotpe, Twelfth Dynasty, in Beni-Hasi, Egypt, shows the royal fowler sitting behind a typical duck blind. His seat, however, is a regal chair, not an old stump. He waits patiently, holding the rope that will spring a trap very similar to those used by English fowlers in the eighteenth century. Meanwhile, a servant fans him so that he may remain cool as he sits out the expectant moment.

Ducks and geese were obviously festive foods in the Nile country. In one of the Egyptian sculpture cases in the Metropolitan Museum of Art, there is a pair of oven-ready, trussed fowl—in marble. This treat, along with several marble jars of vintage wines, was placed in the tomb of the deceased for his refreshment during the long journey to rebirth in the next world.

17. STONE DUCK WEIGHT (SUMERIAN)

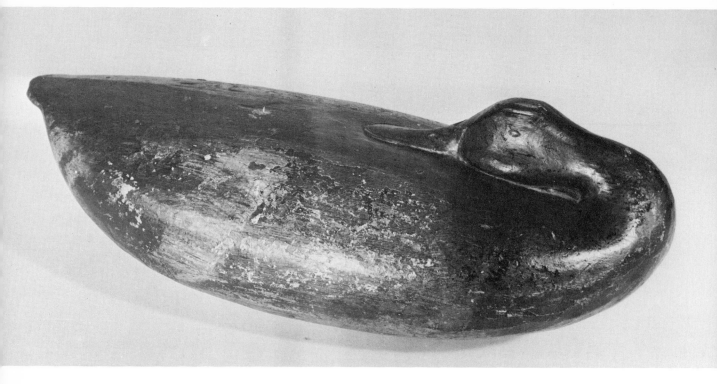

18. BLACK DUCK

There is, however, a Sumerian duck in the Metropolitan Museum that, in its simplicity of form, does resemble a sleeping duck decoy from New England, one cut out of a block of sugar pine. But this ancient duck is a stone weight, not a decoy. It is curious that the sensuous, self-contained forms are so similar, although the artisans were separated by oceans, worlds, and forty centuries of time.

Ducks and all kinds of birds have always been of great decorative interest to artists in the Far East. Japan has a special affinity for all forms of nature. But there is no sign of the decoy in carvings or in prints, although the ducks, heron, and little wading birds that visit our shores are very similar to those seen on the beaches of Japan.

The wildfowl decoy, as a folk art, developed only in America. Only here may one find this sculptural "Audubon" of native birds, in which is represented nearly every species of wildfowl that flew up and down this hemisphere—and some birds that never saw flight at all, except in some man's imagination.

Not all the carvings are good, worth saving, or deserving of the name of "art." Thousands are not—they are simply blocks, awkward and expressionless. The astonishing fact is that so many are excellent—and in almost unbelievable range and variety. There are naturalistic birds, objective represen-

42

tations that are easily identifiable. Others are impressionistic, the actual shapes being modified by the carver's feeling, experience, and sensitivity to birds. Some are highly stylized, and some are primitive. Some have been wrought with infinite pains, others cut casually from pieces of driftwood, fence posts, or ship timbers washed up on the beach.

But it is not the material or the style that matters: It is what happened in the hands of the man who made it. The one question was and is: Does the decoy catch the bird in body and spirit? If it does, we may truly call it art.

Of all our folk arts, none is more strikingly American than the decoy. Indigenous to this country, popular in use, created out of native woods and natural formations—what could be more expressive of the people, their need, and their individuality?

19. YELLOWLEGS DECOY

THE WORLD OF CARVINGS

Plover   Sandpiper   Curlew   Yellowlegs

(Comparative size)

21. SANDPIPER COMING IN TO SHOREBIRD DECOYS

THE WORLD OF CARVINGS

THE TIME HAS COME for the decoys to speak for themselves. The following photographs have been carefully selected to acquaint the reader with the variety and quality of the birds. Few comments are necessary except to identify the species, the provenance, and, when known, the carver. The carvings are grouped into four main categories: Shorebirds; Ducks; Geese; Plumage Birds and Solitary Persuaders.

SHOREBIRDS

The terms "shorebird" and "beachbird" refer to any of the wildfowl that feed along the beaches, the tidal flats, or the lowland marshes and meadows. The word "snipe" is used loosely by hunters to mean any of these small species.

The decoys for these birds are called "stick-ups" because of the practice of mounting them on sticks and setting them in the ground.

The four main groups are: Sandpiper, Yellowlegs, Curlew, and Plover.

Sandpiper

Smallest of the shorebirds are the sandpipers, the gay little creatures so familiar to anyone who has walked along a beach and watched them skittering up and down the tideline, or sunning themselves on the low-lying rocks.

The sandpiper decoy, or "peep," as it is called, can generally be recognized by its small size, from six to eight inches, and by the light breast and speckled back, which is the color of the sand itself—buff, terracotta, and black.

The carvers rarely differentiated between species, inasmuch as several kinds of sandpipers "come in" to the decoy. But they did capture the pert, lively stance common to all varieties.

22. SANDPIPER

23. SANDPIPER ("ROOT-HEAD")

Yellowlegs

Most delicate and varied of all the shorebirds is the lovely yellowlegs, with its graceful, slender contours. The decoys have the light underparts and darkish back of the sandpiper, but they are considerably larger. The bill is longer than that of the "peep" or of the plover.

There are two kinds of yellowlegs: the "lesser," which measures about ten or eleven inches, and the "greater," which may reach sixteen.

24. YELLOWLEGS ON SHORE

25.   LESSER AND GREATER YELLOWLEGS

26.   GREATER YELLOWLEGS, AUDUBON PRINT

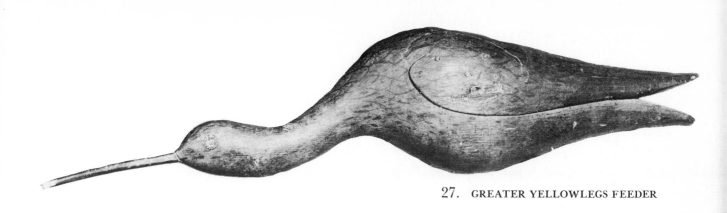

27. GREATER YELLOWLEGS FEEDER

28. GREATER YELLOWLEGS AND SANDPIPER

Curlew

The curlew, largest and most impressive of the shorebirds, has a full, sculptural body and a probing thrust to the beak, which may be as long as eight inches. Its overall color is of cinnamon tones, and its back is flecked with golden-brown and slate accents.

There are three kinds of curlew decoys: the long-billed or sickle-billed (decurved bill) is the largest and may measure some twenty inches; the Hudsonian is distinguished mainly by a dark streak through the eyes on both sides of the head; and the Eskimo is the smallest of the three, about fifteen inches. The Eskimo curlew was called "dough-bird" in the South; when plucked it showed white with fat like dough.

Today, the long-billed decoy is rare, the Hudsonian is found only occasionally, and the Eskimo, because the bird itself is extinct, almost never.

29. LONG-BILLED CURLEW, AUDUBON PRINT

30. HUDSONIAN CURLEW ON BEACH

31. LONG-BILLED CURLEW FEEDER

Plover

The plumpest of the shorebird decoys, the plover, is easily differentiated from its companions, the sandpiper and the yellowlegs, by its chunky build and large head.

There are many kinds of plover decoys, but the black-breasted is the most numerous. There is good reason for this. Although other varieties of plover will come to "the black," "the blacks" will come only to their own. The hunters call it "beetle-head" or "bull-head." This seems unfair, because the black-breasted plover is a dressy bird. It wears the white marking of a headscarf over the forehead and down its breast, which is dark, in marked contrast to the light underparts of other beachbirds. Although it is the largest of the plovers, its beak is short and stout in comparison to that of the yellow-legs and the spectacular, long bill of the curlew. Its back is mottled like those

32. BLACK-BREASTED PLOVER FEEDING

33.   BLACK-BREASTED PLOVER IN SPRING AND FALL PLUMAGE

34.   BLACK-BREASTED PLOVER

of the other beachbirds, but is darker. In the fall, its plumage fades, and it is named, ignominiously, "pale-belly."

The only other plover decoy of any importance is that of the golden. Although similar to the black-breasted, it is both smaller and darker, and its back is conspicuously brushed with golden yellows.

Rarities

Other shorebird carvings, closely related to the four main families but shown separately because of their rarity, include the willet, dowitcher, ruddy turnstone, stilt, godwit, and knot.

35. DOWITCHERS AND SANDPIPERS

36. DOWITCHER FEEDING

37. GODWIT AND YELLOWLEGS

38. RUDDY TURNSTONE

39. WILLETS

40.   BLACK-NECKED STILT

41. KNOT SHOREBIRD

42. DUCKS, DUCKS, DUCKS!

More duck decoys are to be found than any other variety, because they were used far and wide. Ducks migrate along all four of the great transcontinental flyways, whereas shorebirds do not. And wherever a duck flew, there was an ambitious hunter with his lures, sometimes with a rig that numbered several hundred—in contrast to the dozen or so used by the snipe hunter.

Duck decoys have also survived because they were apt to be saved, not burned in bonfires or thrown away like snipe when snipe hunting was forbidden by law. Duck hunting is still legal, in a restricted "take" and season, and this wider and continued use of duck decoys makes an excellent old one much easier to find than that of a shorebird. Duck decoys are also called "coys," "tollers," and "stools." The word "decoy" itself comes from the Dutch word "kooi," meaning cage or trap—a fowling method that dates back at least to ancient Egyptian times.

Unlike the shorebird "stick-ups" propped in the beach sands, the ducks are floating lures that ride at anchor, attached to a seine twine and fastened to a weight that drops to the bottom. Such anchoring allows the bird some semblance of movement and keeps it from getting away. This decoy was thus made to move like a duck as well as look like a duck. It had to balance expertly on the waves without toppling and had to respond naturally to the action of wind. Weights and keels on its bottom acted as stabilizers.

The carver, in building his bird so that it would balance, be compact and sturdy, and display no irrelevant detail, inadvertently met the requirements of good sculpture.

Ducks are divided into three general classes: sea ducks or divers; marsh ducks—also called river ducks; and mergansers.

In the following pages, the several species are represented by one or more outstanding decoys, so that the reader may visualize the wide range both in kind and in individual interpretation. The real-life drawings accompanying many of the photographs will help the collector to identify the species, but their main purpose is to show how the carver translated the actual bird into the sculptural image. If further help is needed in identifying decoys, any authoritative bird guide will list details of beak, eye, head, body conformation, and plumage patterns, as well as male and female differentiations and seasonal change of plumage. Most decoys are drakes, presumably because their feathers are more attractive than those of the hen. Although spring gunning has long been outlawed, nearly all decoys are painted in spring plumage because it is more conspicuous than that of the fall.

43. CANVASBACK

But the collector must not demand exact ornithological detail. The decoyist took many liberties. Simplicity and effectiveness were more important to him than scientific rendering. It was the impression that counted.

Sea Ducks or Divers

Striking white patches on any duck indicate a seabird—nature's way of camouflaging him as he bobs among the whitecaps of the sea. In some sections of the country these ducks are called "whites." The term "sea duck"

44. WHISTLER

does not mean that the bird or its decoy is found only near the sea; it may also frequent deep rivers, bays, or any large body of inland water.

In contrast to the marsh ducks, which inhabit quieter waters and feed on shallow aquatic plants and roots, the sea duck dives for its food and needs a streamlined build—a low tail and sloping watershed back. When fishing or hiding, it can disappear completely, swimming under water and surfacing forty or fifty feet away. Whistlers are often seen in small, gay groups playing "dive and seek" as they splash about in a protected cove. An old squaw can plunge to the unbelievable depth of a hundred feet.

The decoy for the sea duck can be identified both by the predominant white markings and by the low, slanting build; it is made wider in the beam, to ride the rough waters without rolling or pitching.

The sea duck decoys illustrated are the canvasback, whistler, bluebill or broadbill, ring-necked, redhead, bufflehead, scoter, coot, eider, old squaw, ruddy, and grebe.

46. REDHEAD

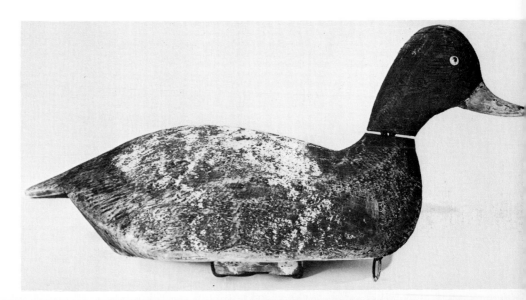

47. BUFFLEHEAD

48. RING-BILLED DUCK

49. EIDER

50. WHITE-WINGED SCOTERS: HEN AND DRAKE

51. COOT

52. RUDDY

53. OLD SQUAW

Marsh Ducks

The marsh duck is the most numerous. It goes under many names. Depending upon where it happens to be, it may be called a river duck, a pond duck, a shoal duck, or very simply, a puddle duck.

Of all the marsh ducks, the mallard is the most important. In fact, it is the most important of all game birds, not only in America but throughout the world. In this country, it flew over nearly every waterway and supplied ample and delicious food for generations of hunters.

Inland birds are usually better eating than sea ducks, which often taste fishy and are usually bypassed if the hunter can take a marsh duck—a vegetarian. It is probable that these birds were also the first to be hunted; no boat was needed, and a man could shoot from the banks and retrieve his game in shallow water, or even on dry land.

The marsh duck decoy, because it is patterned from the shallow diver, can be distinguished from the deep-sea divers by its upturned tail and narrow beam.

The marsh duck decoys illustrated are the mallard, black, pintail, widgeon, green-winged teal, wood duck, and shoveller.

54. GREBE

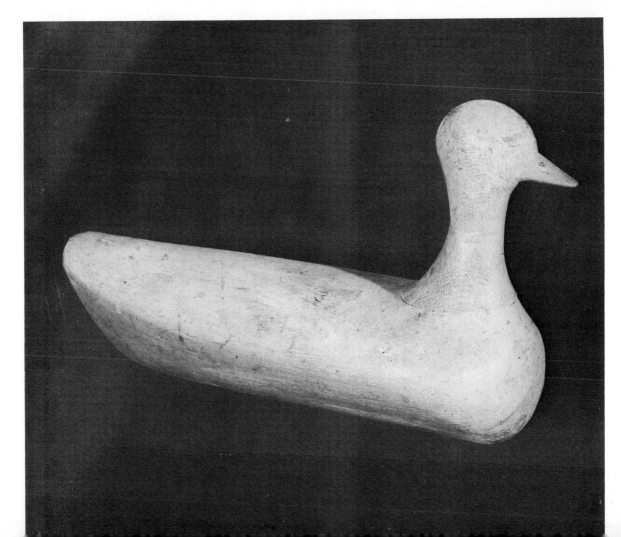

55. BLACK DUCK

56. BLACK DUCK

57. BLACK DUCK

58. WOOD DUCK

59. MALLARD

60. PINTAIL

61. WIDGEON

62. GREEN-WING TEAL

63. SHOVELLER

Merganser or Sheldrake

The merganser is grouped separately by ornithologists and "duckers" because of its rounded, serrated bill, so unlike the flat, laminate bill of other ducks. Its flesh has a rank, fishy flavor—which has been compared to the taste of an old kerosene-lamp wick—and the bird is thus hunted less frequently than the other species.

64. RED-BREASTED MERGANSER

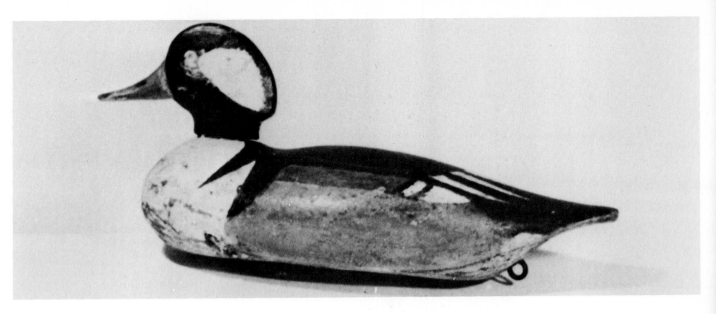

65. HOODED MERGANSER

But the relatively few merganser decoys found are highly prized. With their slim, elegant, crested heads, they are the aristocrats of the decoy family.

The three varieties of merganser decoys are the American merganser, which frequents fresh water; red-breasted merganser; and hooded merganser, the rarest of the family.

66. AMERICAN MERGANSERS: HEN AND DRAKE

One of the most thrilling natural sights is a wedge of Canada geese coming in against a sunset sky, their weaving edge circling and lowering over the dusky marshes, their honking filling the night air with a sound centuries old.

67. FLYING GOOSE
(SIGN ON HUNTING LODGE)

68. CANADA GOOSE

This king of waterfowl, unique to this hemisphere, is widely distributed over North America. Except for the swan and the crane, the Canada goose is the largest of the wildfowl. The decoy is easily recognized by the long "black-stocking" neck, the white cheeks, and the full, brownish-gray body.

69. SLEEPING CANADA GOOSE

Canada Geese

70.   BRANT GOOSE

The only other goose seen in any quantity is the brant. This bird, frequenting the Eastern seaboard between New England and North Carolina, is similar in size to the gull, and it sits like a gull on the water. The decoy for the brant goose is mostly black; its belly is white, and around its neck it wears a white necklace.

71. SNOW GOOSE

Occasionally, one may discover a decoy of the snow goose. A hundred years ago, this bird was a familiar sight everywhere in America; but today it is rarely seen in the East, for its main flight is along the Pacific flyway.

Although I have seen ornamental decoys of the blue goose, the barnacle, and the Hutchins, I have never seen "working" decoys of these birds.

72. SWAN

Many of our most striking decoys—the heron, egret, bittern, crane, swan, and gull—were made primarily for the feather hunters, although a few of these birds were also taken for food. High fashion in ladies' hats from the 1870's to the turn of the century demanded such lavish and exotic trimmings as dyed plumes of all colors, and even the heads of hawks or owls, complete with staring glass eyes and lacquered beaks.

The market price for a pair of gull's wings was eleven cents at Macy's. A sandpiper skin in full feather sold for a cent. Frank Chapman, a society columnist of the 1890's, did some bird-watching one fall afternoon in New York's City Hall Park: He counted forty different specimens of birdlife—fixed on ladies' bonnets.

After legislation prohibited the gunning of wildfowl for their plumage, many of the decoys made for this purpose found other uses—one being that of a "confidence" decoy, a polite name for a stool pigeon. This lone decoy was placed with a group of regulars to give a false sense of security to the scene. For example, it was an old custom to tether a gull decoy with a string of brant, or to set a heron with a flock of yellowlegs. A crane decoy was often employed with geese, since the crane, in real life, acts as a look-out for them while they feed on grains or eel grass.

In other words, birds, being gregarious creatures, will flock not only to birds of their own kind but will also drop by to visit and gabble in any setting that looks congenial.

Actually, the plumage decoys doubled as "confidence" birds even during the permissive days of feather hunting. When the plumage market was out of season, the fowler would extend his income by gunning for the more usual game birds.

All plumage decoys are rare, partly because they were used singly or in small groups rather than in large rafts like the ducks and geese, and partly because the market was not extensive. Feathers sold mainly to the milliners of New York and Philadelphia.

Those areas where plumage birds gathered were also limited. For example, it is primarily along the coastal regions of Long Island and New Jersey that one finds the graceful and dignified heron decoys, including the great blue, the egret, and the bittern. (A fascinating, dismountable, "do-it-yourself" heron is illustrated in the next section.)

73. BLUE HERON

74. BITTERN

84

75. EGRETS

76. GULL

As for the sandhill crane, I know of only two old decoys extant—one from Connecticut, the other from New Mexico. The crane was hunted for food as well as for feathers. There is record of cranes being offered for food in New Orleans in the 1830's; and in the 1880's, when cranes flocked to Minnesota in great numbers and trampled the corn like sheep, they were not only shot, but were stuffed and roasted for the table.

77. SANDHILL CRANE

Legal hunting for the sandhill crane was reinstated in New Mexico in 1961 for the thirty days of November. According to William S. Huey of Santa Fe, crane decoys are in use again today, but of the "stick-up" silhouette type. Mr. Huey states further: "Sandhill cranes are among the most susceptible of birds to the lure of the decoy, but at the same time one of the most difficult of all birds to hunt. The slightest false note in the decoy setup or around the pit will be picked out and rejected by the cranes even before the hunter knows he is being considered."[8]

78. SANDHILL CRANE

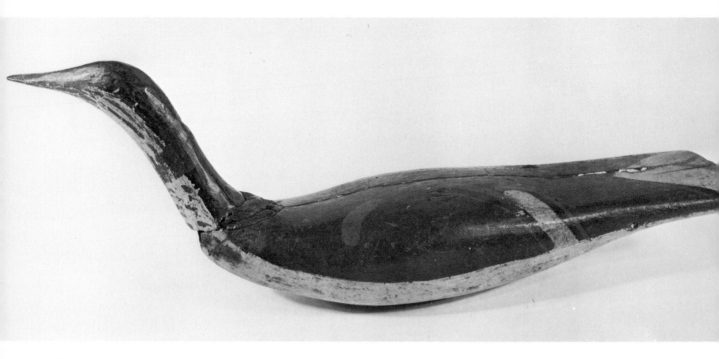

79. LOON

80. CORMORANT

Swan were taken for their down and their feathers; their decoys are found principally along the bays from Maryland to North Carolina. The most famous and traveled swan decoy in America graces the Shelburne Museum collection in Vermont. In 1958, this elegant and tranquil creature journeyed to the Brussels Universal and International Exhibition. The Shelburne catalogue says of it: "An exceptionally rare and beautifully carved Chesapeake Bay swan, it was made by Samuel T. Barnes of Havre de Grace, Maryland, about 1890, for use on the Susquehanna Flats."[9]

Some decoys—such as the loon, the crow, and the owl—are known as "solitary persuaders." The loon has a wary and unsociable nature, and the sight of a single loon swimming contentedly on the tranquil bosom of a lake might well indicate safety to any migrant looking for a secure place to rest.

The exact reason for hunting the loon has never been determined satisfactorily. Its feathers were not distinguished, and it was not generally hunted for food. However, its breast oil reputedly served as a fine oil for the cleaning of guns.

Whatever its special purpose, two of the fairest decoys in the realm are of loons. The one at the Shelburne Museum is carved in a swimming pose. The other, a great northern loon, rests "at ease." Both are superb examples of floating sculpture.

The crow decoy, not to be confused with that of the blackbird, is one of the most sophisticated and witty of all decoys. It saw use as a confidence decoy on the New England beaches, where crows pick over debris left on the sandbars by the receding tide. Presumably, if the beach was safe enough for the crafty crow, it was safe for any passing snipe. But this handsome, jet-black decoy served mostly to keep the fowler's shooting arm in practice when game birds were out of season. There is no closed season on crows.

Few people have a fondness for crows, and the farmer especially hated the devils that ate his seed corn and ruined his harvest. If a scarecrow did not frighten off the scavengers, and if tin cans tied together and clanking in the wind did not "flare" them, he would plant a few decoys in the furrows and fire away at the predators when they came in to investigate.

81.   PRIMITIVE CROWS

82.   SOPHISTICATED CROWS

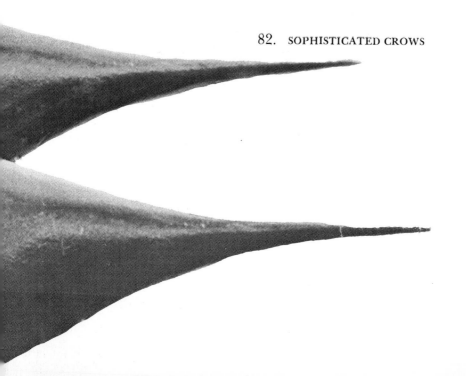

The only known use of the owl decoy was to attract crows, which like to gang up on this bird of prey. The owl in the illustration is hollowed out, so that it can be set on a post or a dead branch. Its large, ominous eyes and tattered leather ears give it the eerie look of the nocturnal world.

83. CROW ON BEACH

Among the other landbirds hunted were the passenger pigeon and the gentle dove. The passenger pigeon was gunned out of existence. A fine and rare pair of decoys, carved by Joseph Coudon of Aiken, Maryland, in the 1870's, shows us what they looked like. Dove decoys are more often found, but they are far from common.

84. OWL

85. PASSENGER PIGEONS

THE USEFUL AND THE BEAUTIFUL

86. THREE METHODS OF
USING SHOREBIRD DECOYS

SNIPE. *Amityville, New York, c. 1830. Found under a boathouse floor.*
(Collection of Malcolm J. Fleming. Photo by Charles R. Meyer.)

HERON. *By Lester Gardner, Amityville, New York, c. 1915.*
(Collection of Malcolm J. Fleming. Photo by Charles R. Meyer.)

CURLEW. *From a rig used by Theodore Rogers at Jamaica Bay, New York, c. 1880.* (*Collection of Malcolm J. Fleming. Photo by Charles R. Meyer.*)

YELLOWLEGS. *From a rig used by Theodore Rogers at Jamaica Bay, New York, c. 1880.* (*Collection of Malcolm·J. Fleming. Photos by Charles R. Meyer.*)

BLUEBILL. *By Ira Hudson, Chincoteague, Virginia, c. 1900.*
(Collection of Harvey Richardson. Photo by Charles R. Meyer.)

CANADA GOOSE. *By Wilbur A. Corwin, Bellport, New York.*
(Collection of Harvey Richardson. Photo by Charles R. Meyer.)

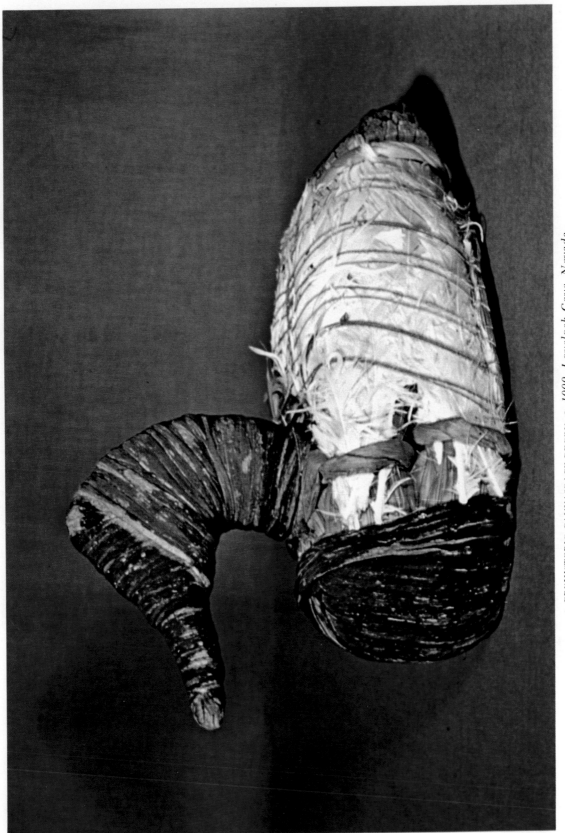

PREHISTORIC CANVASBACK DECOY, c. 1000. Lovelock Cave, Nevada.
(Museum of the American Indian, Heye Foundation, New York City.)

BLUEBILL. *By Caleb Carman, Southhaven, New York, c. 1800.*
(Collection of Malcolm J. Fleming. Photo by Paul W. Bigelow.)

CANVASBACK. *By Lem Ward, Chrisfield, Maryland, c. 1930.*
(Collection of Harvey Richardson. Photo by Paul W. Bigelow.)

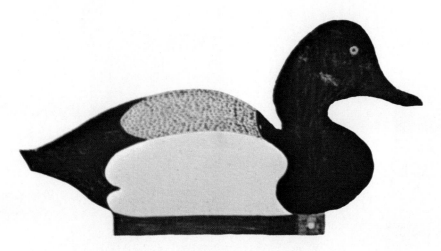

BROADBILL PATTERN. *By Paul W. Bigelow, Bellport, New York.*
(Photo by Paul W. Bigelow.)

CROW. *By Charles H. Perdew, Henry, Illinois.*
(Collection of Malcolm J. Fleming. Photo by Paul W. Bigelow.)

SEAGULL. *By Frank Kellum, Babylon, New York, c. 1890. Used at Wa-Yanda Club, Bayshore, New York, where Kellum was a guide. (Collection of Malcolm J. Fleming. Photos by Charles R. Meyer.)*

THE USEFUL
AND THE BEAUTIFUL

THOUGH THE DECOY is enjoyed mainly for its own sake—for its form, color, and texture—some understanding of hunting practices can increase our pleasure by providing a frame of reference. Decoy-making is a functional art, and the decoy's use on the water or on the beaches had a marked, and salutary, effect on its form.

THE SNIPE HUNTER AND HIS QUIET BIRDS

The use of the snipe decoy was a simple undertaking, in contrast to the intricacies of hunting with the larger, floating decoys of ducks and geese. The shorebird hunter merely propped his "stick-ups" on the beaches or on the tidal flats and waited. When the surf receded, the sandpipers, the plover, and all the visiting migrants came in to snatch their edibles—the tiny wet crabs, the hoppers, and the sandworms.

The fowler took care to arrange his lures in as natural and lively a manner as possible, like a stage set—which indeed it was. He usually selected a variety of species, to give an impression of authenticity. A few sanderlings might be placed running along the tideline in company with a dowitcher, and perhaps a scattering of plover would be set upbeach near the grasses. To make the scene even more realistic, the meticulous fowler would select birds posed in different attitudes of running, eating (called "feeders"), sleeping, or even dozing. Sometimes he helped his cause by whistling the birds down, by imitating the wild call of the plover or the three-note cry of the yellowlegs.

A rare photograph of a working snipe rig, taken in 1905, shows several varieties of shorebirds, including a willet and two curlew, the latter made by the old Mason Decoy Company. The rig belonged to Wendall Squire of Hampton Bays, Long Island.

The snipe hunter, after placing his decoys, did not have to hide in the grasses or behind a stump as carefully as the "ducker" did. Shorebirds are bolder than ducks. If he sat quietly, they came cascading out of the sky as if out of nowhere, dropping onto the sands, chattering as they probed in and out among the wooden decoys, and leaving behind a playful network of footprints that were soon softly erased by the sea.

It seems unbelievable that men went through all this effort of making the decoy, traveling to the beaches, and waiting for the quarry simply to eat these birds. They are so little. But plover pie was a delicacy. The birds were plucked, braised, seasoned, and cooked with carrots and onions under a flaky crust. And the aroma of juicy, plump curlew roasting on a whirly spit was a satisfying reward for the weariest of hunters.

Another reason for taking the little shorebirds was their early appearance. They migrate first, before the larger birds come. In the spring, the

87. SNIPE RIG

yellowlegs appear at about the time the first peep frog is heard and when the willows show green. And in the fall, the shorebirds come through on their southward journey as early as August, while the hardy black duck still loiters in the northern ponds.

The carving and the whittling of the snipe decoy was done mostly at home, in the basement or the shed. The only necessary tool was a jackknife, and the job was usually a casual affair, although some men were as painstaking as if they were making a fine cabinet. For material, they used whatever was handy—a block of wood, a fence post, a cedar root.

They knew their woods. Aged wood was best—it didn't split if cut with the grain. And the weathered pieces of wood naturally acquired tones of silver and brown that helped to evoke the look and feel of feathers without the necessity of using paint.

89. SANDPIPERS OF WOOD,
     TIN, CORK, AND LEATHER

"Found" material was always popular with the frugal baymen, who appreciated a saving of time and material. It was always possible to pick up driftwood from the beach—a piece that had a provocative shape and might be whittled into a bird. Cork from life preservers and fish-net buoys was also gathered up, taken home, and worked into shapely snipe. The texture, lightness, and brownish color of cork adapts itself sympathetically to the look and feel of a bird.

Newspapers and brown paperbags—materials available to everyone— were made into a kind of papier-mâché bird. My own collection includes a "lesser" yellowlegs made from a Civil War daily. The pieces had been cut to a pattern, pasted together, and moulded; they were held together by some kind of waterproof adhesive. In mending a torn piece of the bird, I was able to decipher a few fragmented words: ". . . and McCl——n's forces moved ——th along the Antietam."

90. WOOD PATTERNS FOR SNIPE AND DUCKS

The wonderful heron that can be taken apart and put together again looks as if it were made of two broom handles, two wooden balls, and a lobster-pot buoy. Under the tail of this decoy is written in blue pencil: "George Martin's crane, Barnegat, June 1907." In New Jersey, herons were sometimes called cranes, and this bird is certainly a heron.

A sandpiper, made out of leather scraps and put together like a child's rag doll, is a unique item among my decoys. The two halves are sewn with linen thread, then turned inside out, stuffed with sawdust, and sealed. It may have been a child's plaything, but it may equally have been a novel kind of decoy. I don't know.

The easiest decoys for the hunter to carry to the beaches were the silhouette decoys, or "profiles." They were thin, and they stacked easily. Many were of tin, turned out by the local tinsmiths, but most were of wood, bench-cut from paper or wood patterns.

92. HERON SECTIONS

The set of snipe patterns illustrated could have been used for either silhouette or contour birds. The penciled notations indicate that the owner was preparing to make three-dimensional birds.

Decoys in the round are more attractive to birds—and to people—than the profile types. I often wonder what birds must have thought when they saw a whole spread of silhouettes disappear at the moment they flew over them.

Whatever the material—wood, paper, cork, leather, or tin—it was the head of the decoy that received the most attention from the carver. The conformation and the set had to be right, though eye markings were considered unnecessary by most early decoyists. After all, a bird flying at an altitude of several hundred feet can hardly distinguish eye details. Sometimes, just a simple indentation scribed the eye, or often the sides of the head were curved gently to suggest the shaded, concave seat of the eye. Later, tack eyes appeared, and eyes made from shoe buttons, or beads, or glass pinheads. Early in the twentieth century the glass eyes used by taxidermists became available.

The two-piece snipe—head and body made separately and tenoned together—allowed more expression in the set of the head than the one-piece models. The two-piece birds had another advantage: They were easier to

93. DOWITCHERS

repair. It is much simpler to replace a shattered neck section than to make a whole new bird. When one realizes that the fowler toted these decoys hodge-podge in a sack, or laced them on a cord flung over his shoulder, then propped them in the salt spray, wind, and rain, and—as a climax—shot over them, it is a wonder that any are left.

The beak was the most vulnerable part, en route or on target. It had to be tough, made out of a hardwood such as locust or oak. The thrust, as well as the length and the thickness, had to be correct. An indestructible beak was an old nail bent properly, a knitting needle out of the wife's sewing basket, or a piece of whale bone. Rarely does one find an original beak in an old bird.

The wings of the snipe are usually treated as part of the general body contour, and marked—if at all—by a low-relief cut or by a simple painted line. Occasionally one finds that the wing tips are carved distinct from the body, feathered, and even crossed in the back. Often, a little "weep hole" is left between the end feathers, to allow the water to drain off. The tail may receive extra attention, and be split, flared, or grooved. But the older decoyists did not indulge in extraneous carving, in decoration for decoration's sake.

94. YELLOWLEGS

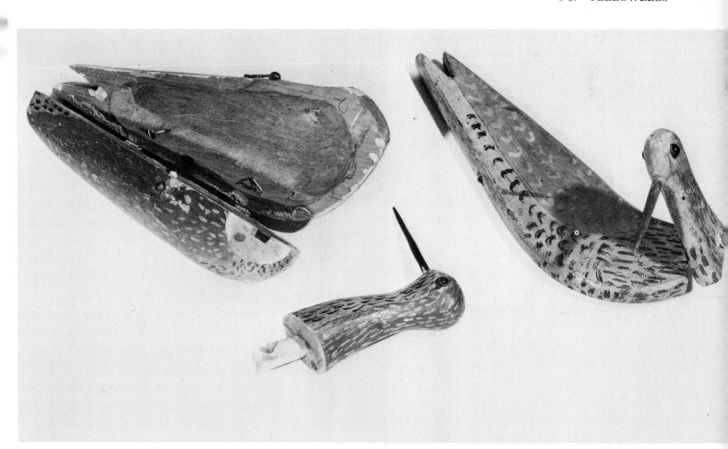

No description of the material and design of the shorebird decoy would be complete without a look at the ingenious experimental birds. Almost every outdoorsman dreams that he can make a better trap, a better trout fly —or a better decoy. And he tries.

One Yankee, unfortunately anonymous, tried very hard; he was a beautiful craftsman. Of his two experimental yellowlegs shown, one is a full-bodied bird, carved in two half-sections and hollowed out. These halves are so hinged with little brass wires that the body of the bird may open and close like a box. The head is separate, detachable, and of a size that can fit inside the bird for protection when the decoy is not in use. His other yellowlegs is a silhouette. Its head is on hinges and can be folded flat against the body of the bird, thus protecting the fragile beak. Fine feather-painting decorates both birds.

95. BLACK-BREASTED PLOVER WITH MOVABLE WINGS

Action birds seemed like a good idea to many a man—a bird that could move and attract attention by turning in the wind, or wiggling its head, or flapping its wings. Another unknown craftsman made a black-breasted plover with metal wings that could be raised and lowered by a cord held in the hand of the hunter as he hid in the bushes.

Another invention was mobile—a yellowlegs stick-up that could turn, always facing into the wind as a good bird should. It is hollow and of one piece, and its belly is left open so that it can catch the wind and move in

96. YELLOWLEGS

much the same way as a windsock on an airfield. The bird itself looks and feels like a shell, delicate but strong. Its eyes are amethyst.

But most inventions were more fanciful than practical. The average carver trusted the quiet bird that could create the *illusion* of movement.

Only one technical problem faced every carver of the snipe. It was necessary to locate the correct balance point for drilling the prop-hole in the base of the bird—the hole into which the prop-stick was inserted. If the decoy did not balance properly, it would swing and sway and behave in a manner unbecoming a bird. Several holes drilled in the bottom of a bird betray a desperate man.

Once in a while one finds a decoy with a single wire leg—or sometimes, two. These are usually early decoys. But it is easy to see why such permanent metal legs were not as popular as the removable sticks. They were a nuisance to carry in the decoy sack.

Decoy construction is as various as the great variety of men who made them. Differences in craftsmanship, line of trade, knowledge of the winged ones, individual temperament, locale, choice of material—all had their influence. And no matter how long one studies the work of these hunter-craftsmen, it is clear that any good bird is much more than the sum of its parts and, in the end, really defies analysis.

97. EGRETS

Duck hunting is still one of the most thrilling sports—though there are not as many ducks as there once were. The method of hunting itself has not changed appreciably in the last hundred years, except that battery shooting has been outlawed. In this ruthless practice, a heavy fixed gun was used; it rested on a revolving crutch in the boat, and the fowl were shot while sitting or rising from the water.

Today, point shooting or flight shooting is favored. The hunter stations himself at a point over which he expects the birds to pass at sunrise or sunset, as they leave or approach their feeding grounds:

It is not my intention to describe wildfowl hunting in detail. The use of blinds, pits, sink boxes, and the various kinds of shooting punts and sculling boats is fully covered in books for the sportsman. But for the nonhunter, a description of the hunter's practices can bring to life in vivid fashion the functional value and importance of the decoy.

The night before the opening of the duck season, the hunter moves into his favorite grounds, so that he may be ready by dawn. Perhaps he scans the skies and tests the wind before he goes to bed. If he is well acquainted with the neighborhood, he will try to find out what kind of duck has been flying through—and precisely where.

Sink Box Shooting

L. S.

In the morning, in the dark before dawn, the hunter is out, paddling or rowing into the open water, which is often rough and squally in November. Stormy weather, which makes the birds feel restless and puts them on the move, provides some of the best hunting. The hunter must set his rig and hide himself before it is light, and before the birds are in the sky.

Each wooden "stool," already weighted with lead and wrapped with seine twine or a tarred cod line, is tossed overboard into the icy water. Ordinarily, decoys are not placed close to the position where the hunter will hide. They are set so that the ducks can swing in to them without the necessity of passing over the blind. The direction of the wind must also be considered; a diving duck will "toll," or come in, against the wind.

The "tollers," or decoys, are not just scattered on the water. They are placed in a pattern—in an irregular string, or in a V-shaped formation. One strategy is to divide them into two groups, allowing a space between them for the birds to alight.

As to the number used, a single shoal gunner may carry from six to twelve, but the open-water man takes more—twenty or thirty. The number also depends on the kind of bird anticipated. It takes a great number of stools to interest the canvasback and the redhead.

After the fowler has placed his decoys to his satisfaction, he returns to shore. He takes cover in his duck blind or he conceals himself in his boat and waits. Once he is in hiding, no movement must betray his presence, no white handkerchief blowing a cold nose, no glint of gun, no bottled spirits, no tossed cigarette paper, no smoke. His self-control must be as complete as that of an anchorite.

And then, in the flat-gray light through which he has been moving like a wraith, a soft glow appears low on the horizon. It spreads and spreads, tossing gold and crimson arches across the sky. The mists on the water clear, and the sun of a new day rises as clean and surprising as if it were the first day of creation.

One of the pleasures of the hunter is his sense of escape from the noisy confusions of the manmade world, and of becoming part of the primitive pattern—the eternal rhythms of day and night, ebb tide and flood tide, the coming and going of the birds.

His day is complete if he sees that telltale wisp of cloud appear, that curl which grows and grows into a plume of mallards moving in across the bay. If the wild ones see his decoys and break and plummet before him, and if his gun drops one bird, he is satisfied. Like the Indian before him, he has matched wits with nature—and won.

The Carving of the Decoy

The actual carving and preparation of the duck decoys took place in winter, when the men were home, the boats beached, the crops in, the fences cleared, and the firewood stacked by the kitchen door.

In some ways, the "ducker" had an easier job of carving than did the snipe-carver. The greater size of the duck permitted him to work out details on a larger scale. There was also more opportunity to experiment. At the same time, a more rugged construction was necessary, because these decoys had to withstand both rough usage in the boats and long exposure to water and weather.

The methods of putting a bird together differed from man to man, and from region to region, but most decoyists used the same basic procedure. This was first described to me one winter afternoon on Cape Cod by the widow of an old-time carver whom I shall call "Captain Preston." (Use of the real name would bring an army of unwelcome collectors to his widow's door—and the actual name, by the way, is not Crowell.)

I had heard about the Captain's decoys, but I had never seen any. That afternoon, "Mrs. Preston" had been reminiscing about the good old days before the building of Route 6 and the flood of summer tourists—the days when the Captain was still with her. Suddenly she turned to me and asked if I would like to see some of his decoys. I nodded enthusiastically, and her daughter was at once dispatched to the cellar with instructions to bring up "that old clothes basket." The girl disappeared down a trap door under the kitchen table. A few moments later she reappeared, struggling with a basket full of ducks. One look at those distinctive heads and horsehair crests poking over the rim of the basket, and I knew they were beauties—mergansers.

The birds were taken out of their nest one by one and set in a circle on the pine floor, their buoyant shapes seeming to float in the winter sunlight. Mrs. Preston had not seen them since her husband passed away many years earlier, and she looked at them as lovingly as most people regard their family silver. She explained that they had been hidden "below decks," not because she didn't like them, but because she didn't want the neighborhood boys asking to shoot over them. She knew she could not say "no."

She talked about the Captain, his pride in the birds, and how hard he had worked over them. In the spring, he carefully selected the wood—good, clear pine blocks, two by sixes, about fourteen inches long. This allowed the long summer for drying and seasoning. Then, in the fall, when his boat was beached, he began his "inside work."

First, the prime block was secured in a vise and the general shape roughed out with a drawknife. Then, he used his horn-handled jackknife to refine the surfaces and model the gently sloping back and tail. The head was cut separately from a wood pattern saved from one season to the next—and from father to son. This unit was doweled into the body with all the neatness of a cabinet-maker's skill. Finally, the whole bird was sandpapered smooth.

When it came time to paint, the Captain did not use any old can of leftovers that happened to be in the boathouse at the end of summer. He bought fresh white lead for the basecoat and mixed his own finish colors for the feathercoat: soft greens, reds, and ochre for the stippling of the breast. The final touch, after the paint had dried and the shine had been rubbed down, was the insertion of the eyes and the crest. The eyes were said to be of the famous "Sandwich" glass made right there on the Cape. The distinctive merganser headdress was supplied by hairs from a horse's tail, tied into tiny bunches and inserted into holes punched along the crown of the head.

The finished carving was wrapped in an old sailcloth and put away until spring, when the rigging was applied—a two-ounce lead attached at the bottom, and the anchor line fastened to a leather loop at the front.

Before the mergansers saw action, they got a trial run in the rain barrel. If the birds kept an even keel and looked lifelike in the barrel's waves, the Captain 'lowed they were ready to "go over."

98.   RED-BREASTED MERGANSERS, WITH CLOSE-UP OF HEAD

Regional Designs and Devices

From a hunter's point of view, a good decoy handled easily, adapted itself well to local water and weather conditions—and pulled in the birds.

The rough seas of the North Atlantic require mammoth decoys, outsized and heavy. The water off Newfoundland and Maine moves endlessly in the deep flow of the tides, even on a calm day, and on this turbulent surface small decoys could not be seen.

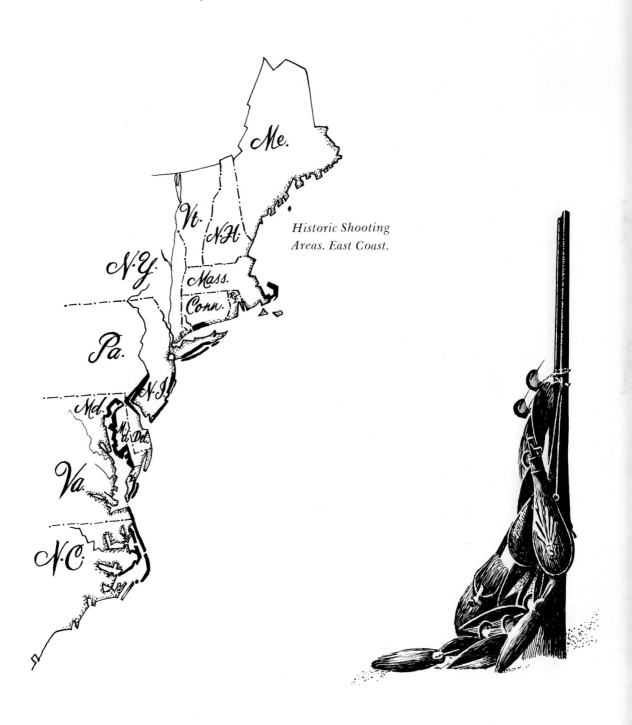

Historic Shooting Areas. East Coast.

99.   LONG ISLAND "REACHERS," "TIP-UPS," AND A DELAWARE MALLARD

100. LIVE GEESE "REACHERS" AND "TIP-UPS"

The heroic eider duck from Cape Porpoise, Maine, is an ideal example of the Northern coy. It is built to ride high in the water, with its head wedged back so that it will not upset in a sudden squall. The breast is flat and broad, serving as a bumper against ice and as a balance against the downward tug of the anchor line. The painting on the bird is a black and white wave, as bold and simple as a wave in a Japanese print. Its purpose is to be seen. In the illustration of the eider, both sides are shown. One is the weathered half of the bird as it looked when found; the other has been repainted to indicate how this handsome decoy looked originally. Wooden pegs clinch the bird together.

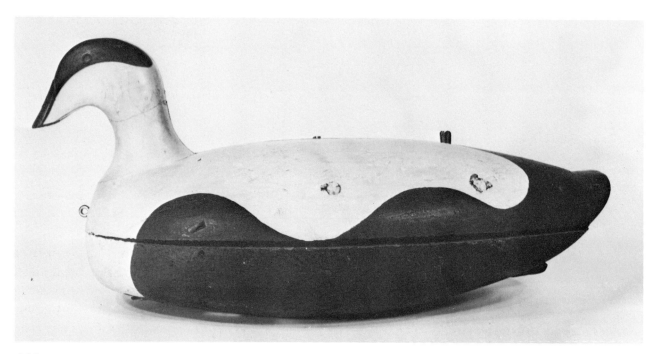

101. EIDER

102. EIDER

The eider duck was hunted for food and not, as many people believe, for its down. Although its flesh is tough and stringy, hashed eider mixed with potatoes and onions can be appetizing on a frosty night. Most of the down for pillows and comforters was obtained by robbing the eider nests perched along the rocky ledges of the shore. The mother duck plucks her own breast to line the nest for her eggs. She makes this lining large enough to be folded over inside, as a comforter to keep her young warm after they are hatched.

The "frame" sea coot was another large, showy decoy from New England. Along Massachusetts Bay these coot decoys were built on the lobster-pot principle—an open frame covered with double canvas and painted black. The result was a bulky but light and conspicuous decoy weighing only five or six pounds.

The "slat goose" is illustrative of another ingenious way of obtaining size without weight. Longitudinal slats, preferably of bass wood, about four feet long, made up the body, and the carved head, prominent and erect, was attached. One such "slat goose" was nailed at each corner of a large, triangular float, creating an impressive trio. Sometimes the slats were not covered by canvas; this open frame allowed the wind to blow through the geese without upsetting them. The great rigs were so cumbersome that they were left out all season.

Jo Lincoln, of Accord, Massachusetts, made dozens of these huge decoys, and he carved heads for many more, which he gave to his neighbors. Jo preferred to call them "barrel geese" and found them most effective when used in conjunction with live decoys. In his day, "honkers" were still legal.

Another construction typical of the North Atlantic was the "shadow duck" decoy. This was a silhouette cut out of wood and mounted at the ends of a board, or often on two boards in a cross hatch, and then floated. "Shadow ducks," as well as "slat geese," have been shot over in New England for a hundred and fifty years.

103.   MASSACHUSETTS SEA COOT

Maine Wildfowling with Shadow Decoys

Old Squaw Shadow Decoys

Slat Goose

South of Massachusetts, the next famous gunning area in New England lies along the Housatonic River of Connecticut, especially in the Stratford area, where the river flows into Long Island Sound. The wild fowl migration here follows the southerly direction of the river, and for some unknown reason many ducks that are flying a more easterly course head inland for the Housatonic after passing over the tip of Long Island.

The decoys made for the protected waters of this river do not require the bulk of ocean decoys. They are smaller and lighter in weight. Even hollow decoys, or those made of cork, are practical here. But there was slush ice in the river to contend with, and so decoys of this region carry a full, prominent breast, and the head is withdrawn, with little or no neck showing. I have been told that bacon rind was rubbed over the beaks and the fronts of the Housatonic birds to prevent icing.

The home of the cork decoy was Long Island. The first ducker known to have worked in cork was Wilbur R. Corwin of Bellport, whose decoys date from about 1850. Cork, which has continued in popular use to the present, was readily available from building suppliers as well as from the beaches, and its color and texture, especially when sanded and charred, looked very much like the soft feathering of the black duck—the most important waterfowl of Great South Bay.

The Long Island decoys are generally solid, with one notable exception. Only hollow decoys were practical on the light ice boats built for the thrilling and dangerous sport of ice gunning in the open water holes.

104. CHESAPEAKE BAY CANVASBACKS

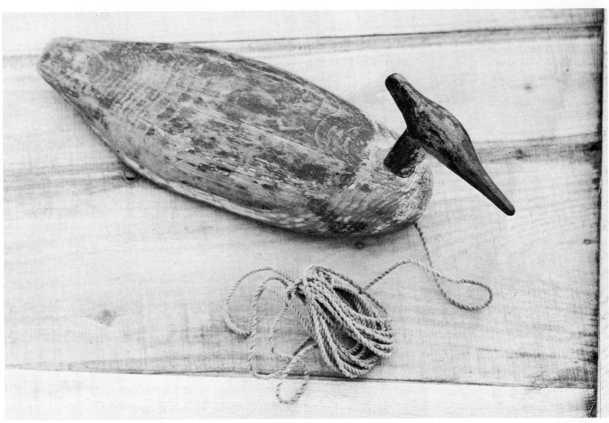

105. AMERICAN MERGANSER ("ROOT-HEAD")

Another distinguishing characteristic of the Long Island decoy was the use of natural roots and tree knots for the heads of ducks, heron, and snipe. In an off season, the natives combed the woods for likely shapes of windswept pine and cedar. They gathered them in sacks, carried them home, and in the long winter evenings they steamed them and shaped them into decoy heads that could later be sold to the fowlers. These "knot-heads" were not only lifelike, but they were tough. The oldest merganser I own is a Long Island root-head, dating from the late eighteenth century.

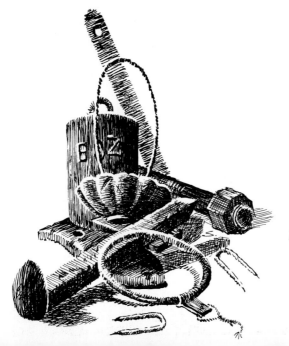

Decoy Weights

121

Long Island Hunter with Heron Decoy

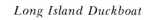
Long Island Duckboat

If one continues down the coastline, as the bird flies, the next port of call is Barnegat Bay, New Jersey, which lies directly in the path of the Atlantic flyway and offers fifty miles of protected inland water and marsh for feeding and resting. The decoys used in the northern end of the bay are solid—the deep water there allows the use of heavy boats and heavy decoys.

But below Chadwick, where the bay shallows, lighter boats and hollow decoys are practical. These decoys are usually cedar and about the same size as the bird itself. The usual practice was to split a log lengthwise with an axe, gouge out the halves, and rejoin them. This joint, nearly center, accounts for the pleasing oval shape of these birds.

107. ILLINOIS PINTAIL

Sculling on the Delaware

Bordering New Jersey on the west is the Delaware River, where the duck hunter has developed a hunting technique that calls for a special decoy. He sculls down on the birds as they rest on the water, not following the usual practice of flight shooting from a blind or a duck boat.

According to local theory, the decoys of the upper Delaware must be realistically carved and painted and be much more likelife than ordinary decoys; they must continue to fool the wild birds at close range, holding them on the water after they have come in. It is not surprising, therefore, to find that these birds have been carved with greater attention to feathering. The tails are often splayed or fluted, and the wings raised in a characteristic pose. It is worth noting that stools from the lower Delaware Bay tend to conform to the regular New Jersey models.

To the duck hunter, the words "Chesapeake" and "canvasback" are almost synonymous. Generations of hunters have enjoyed feasting on the spectacular and delectable "can," which, floating in rafts of thousands, winters off the shores.

The bay itself is as vast as a sea, and the tides run heavy. Here, the decoys had to be large, wide of beam and solid, and they are handsome, clean-cut birds of generous proportions. The bottom may be rounded in shape, raked, or strongly V-cut. The earlier decoys from this region carry low heads; the later ones show a high head. At the southern end of the bay, on the Maryland side, a distinctive, wide, flat-bottomed decoy is found, characteristic of a whole group of carvers centered around Chrisfield, Maryland.

The next historic gunning area along the Atlantic flyway includes the islands off Virginia and the broad, open waters of Currituck Sound, and

Pamlico—inland from Hatteras. The decoys of this region are rugged and bold. Many are oversized; some are hollow, some solid. They were made by men like the famous Cobbs and Dudleys—men who did not have much time to fuss, but who knew their birds and knew what worked. Most of the decoys from this area are mere blocks, but the best have the "look" of the authoritative decoy and are prized items.

Many birds winter off the coast of the Carolinas, especially the canvasbacks, redheads, and blacks. Louisiana is a favorite gathering place for those who travel on to more tropical climes. Here, one would expect to find many fine old decoys. But there are almost none. Even recent decoys made out of balsa or cypress root are scarce, though now and then one may come across silhouette goose decoys used in the flats of the Mississippi Delta.

108. LOUISIANA DECOYS: TEAL, BLUEBILL, AND MALLARDS

109. STAMP OF OWNERS

An interesting group of old canvasback, scaup, teal, and mallard decoys came from Avery Island, which lies just at the edge of the Gulf of Mexico. On the bottom of each stool is stamped "McI. Co.," imposed over "CWW." The "McI." stands for McIlhenny, one of the two families who have owned Avery Island since 1770. The "CWW" stamped on the birds is the brand of Charles Willis Ward, an eastern friend who used to shoot on the island with the McIlhennys. This family gave a large tract of land to the state of Louisiana to be used as a waterfowl reservation.

The McIlhenny ducks illustrated are of unpainted cypress. It is the custom in Louisiana to strip off the paint at the end of the hunting season in order to repair the birds. Then they are repainted in the spring.

Avery Island is known for its fine gunning, for its tabasco sauce, and for its rock salt deposit, the oldest in America. It is also the protected winter home of thousands of blue geese.

Leaving the Mississippi Delta and traveling north along the river, one finds few old decoys before reaching the waterways of the Missouri, the Ohio, and the Illinois. And even here, where the migrating flocks from along the great rivers join together at the Mississippi, old decoys are hard to find.

But the first years of the twentieth century produced decoys in quantity. By this time, the manufactured decoy was purchasable and popular, and the "company" designs—both workable and good—inspired many a home carver in his own work. In fact, many hunters did a little side business of their own. They made decoys for sale as well as for their own use. The majority were typical round-bottomed river decoys. Some were hollow, some solid, some oversized, some undersized; some better, some worse. You paid your money and you took your choice.

126

Further north, and to the east, in upper New York State, there is another important fowling region. On the eastern shore of Lake Ontario, thousands of birds congregate on a stopoff between Canada and the South. It is said that a flight of mallards can make the long trip from the Great Lakes to the Gulf in one hop, with time out only for occasional, quick dips to moisten their drying feet in the cool waters of the rivers. But this observation may have been dreamed up by frustrated hunters who returned home empty-handed.

Decoys from this lake area are distinctive. Even the crude ones have character. Many are feather-carved, not in an attempt at realism, but to cut down the reflection of light, which scares off a bird.

Flat, wide bottoms also characterize the decoys of this region. The Great Lakes can kick up a storm as furious as that of an ocean, and a broad beam on a decoy helps it to ride out the breakers. The heads of these decoys tend to be high, to make them more readily visible and to prevent icing. Several interesting, individual types developed in special areas of this region. For example, there is the Alexandria Bay Long Neck, as well as the Ogdensburg Humpback.

The final touch in the construction of all duck decoys—no matter where they were made—was the rigging: the attachment of the anchor line and the weight. The weight on the bottom of the bird lowered its center of gravity and helped to balance it on the water. The size of the weight and its position—front or back—was determined by the special need of each decoy. A weight placed at the rear, like those on Chesapeake canvasbacks, helped to counterbalance the downward pull of the front anchor line. It also prevented the heavy head of the decoy from drinking water.

The weight itself was usually a piece of scrap metal—lead, an old bolt, a horseshoe, a piece of rake. The really careful decoyist, however, went to some trouble to countersink his weight, so that it did not get in the way of the seine twine or "stringer," which was attached to the front of the decoy by a ring or a leather loop, and wrapped around the bird when not in use.

A man like Harry Shourdes of New Jersey would cut a neat rectangle in the base of his decoy, pour lead into the opening, and finish it off flush with the base of the bird. Once in a while, for a personal touch, the decoyist moulded the lead in the shape of a fish or a star.

Occasionally, and not as often as a decoy collector might wish, the carver scribed his initials on the bottom, not as a matter of pride, but as proof of ownership. Decoys got away in a storm, and they were often borrowed and sometimes stolen.

110. BLACK DUCK

111. BROADBILL (GREATER SCAUP)

As we have seen, the initials might be branded on the bird or incised deeply with a knife. A fascinating phase of the search for decoys is to find birds that are signed—and then, to try to figure out the signature! The better-known initials, like the LD of the Lee Dudleys, and the N's and E's of the Cobbs, are worth their weight in silver. But such definite labeling is rare. The inked names found on the bottom of some decoys were usually placed there by a collector trying to establish their identity. However, Lem Ward does sign his name in ink, by request. But it is pretty hard to catch most of the old-time decoy-carvers. They aren't around any more.

A signature may be misleading. Owners put their names on decoys, too, and the owner was not necessarily the carver. In fact, few decoys were signed by their makers. Identification is usually made, therefore, by the style of the carver rather than by any signature.

The duck hunter, like the snipe hunter, has always realized that a little action and some lifelike noise help to catch the attention of passing birds: thus, the inventive "action" decoys. Especially after law prohibited the use of live ducks and geese as decoys, the fowlers were impelled to devise movement and sound for their tollers.

A quacking duck was patented, its voice activated by a bellows and a reed built into the bill. Ducks with bobbing heads and fluttering wings also appeared. Many attempts were made to get the decoy to swim by means of built-in clockworks or power from an onshore battery. Ducks and geese with spread wings were fairly common. These were propped on high, flexible sticks set in a marsh, or they were strung to slide down a wire on signal. But most of these inventions, more ingenious than productive, were short-lived.

The Painted Bird

It has not been scientifically established just how much color a bird actually sees. Some people believe that a bird is practically color blind. Others swear that redhead ducks will respond to the waving of a red handkerchief as surely as men and beasts react to this brilliant color.

But whatever a bird's color sensitivity may be, its vision is vastly keener than man's. The eyes are placed to the side of the head, and the cornea has a wide curvature—wider than man's. The result is truly panoramic vision. In addition, the completely mobile neck allows a bird to look backward as easily as forward.

And yet, no matter what a bird's visual capacity may be, the height and speed at which it travels make it unlikely that it can perceive much color detail on a grounded decoy. Sandpipers have been seen by airplane pilots

Simple Scratch While Paint Is Wet

Comb Painting

Feather Blending

at ten thousand feet, and canvasbacks have been clocked at a good sixty miles an hour.

It is reasonable to conclude that color detail on a decoy plays its part only after the wildfowl have been attracted by its mass and shape, and swing earthward to take a closer look.

Painting the decoy to make it conspicuous as well as to identify its species brought up a novel problem for the decoyist. If he followed nature's plumage pattern of camouflage, the result was hardly conspicuous—at least, to a bird. What method of painting should be used?

Practices varied widely. Some men gave great attention to painting detail, as much to please themselves, it would seem, as to attract the bird. Basic to all methods, however, was the fact that the painting consisted of two coats: an undercoat to seal the wood against weather and waterlogging, and a feathercoat to identify the species. White lead mixed with turpentine was the usual basecoat, although some men preferred to bathe the birds in hot linseed oil as a sealer.

The second coat, in its simplest form, was a rudimentary wash—a mixture of the main, overall body tones. Gray and brown paint were essentials, with white used for lightening and accenting the color. The result was an efficient decoy.

Slat Goose

Most hunters did not have time to fuss with detail or special brush-work and thought it unnecessary. They knew that the main purpose of the second coat was to accent the key features of the bird. Distance-viewing of any object has the advantage of simplifying and consolidating the patterns, and the decoyist painted what he saw. Instinctively, he did what the professional painter learns consciously through the application of visual rules.

This natural simplification, this emphasis on key features—almost to the point of caricature—is clearly illustrated in the decoy of the whistler

112. CANVASBACK PAINTING

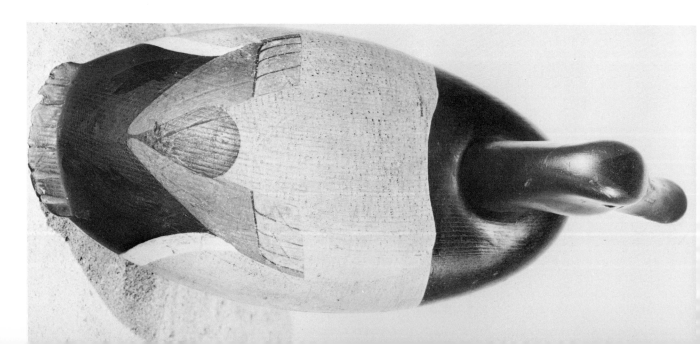

attributed to T. Smith of New Jersey. The head is oversized, accented only by the two dominant white cheek spots; the body is a simple oval, painted with dramatic black and white areas, which are formalized and juxtaposed.

In the hands of the very talented painters like Joseph Dawson, the key color patterns of the feathers emerge in a beautiful, formal design—of interest in itself. The painting of the merganser by Lothrop T. Holmes has such an elegant and elaborate precision that it recalls the formality of ancient oriental paintings. Joseph W. Lincoln's wood duck shows a stylization worthy of a primitive dance mask.

None of these men worked consciously to develop such handsome, stylized forms. They simply sought an attractive method of obtaining results. Many an unschooled bayman worked out painterly answers that professionals do not discover in a lifetime.

Along with the stylist, there was the realist. Elmer Crowell, who worked to simulate the depth and softness of feathering, was a master in this art.

113. AMERICAN MERGANSER: HEN

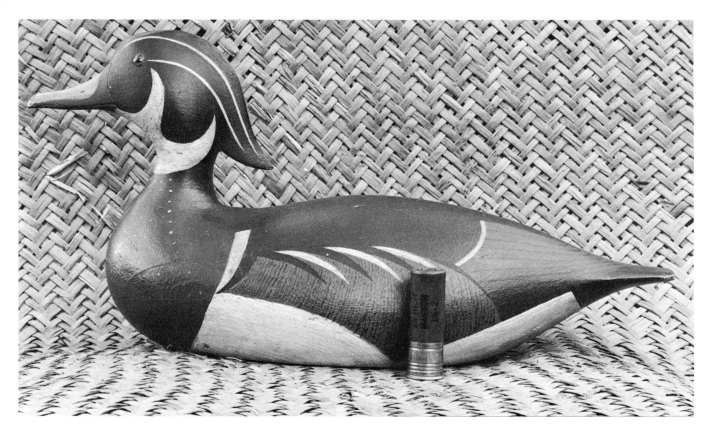

114. WOOD DUCK

115. TWO YELLOWLEGS

116. OLD SQUAW

Each decoyist had his own ideas about translating what he saw into paint, and the variations are limitless. Often, a bird is painted so differently by different men that it is hard to believe it is the same species. Compare the dressy old squaw by Chris Sprague with the stark simplicity of the same bird by Captain I. Clarence Bailey.

117. OLD SQUAWS

The colors of the birds are taken naturally from those of the earth and the sea, the river banks, and the marsh grasses. Lem Ward's palette of dominant browns, blue-grays, olive-greens, and blacks reflect these tones, and, interestingly enough, are similar to the color combinations used by the great French painter Georges Braque. But I am sure that Lem has never heard of Braque. His sense of color is intuitive, and his natural feeling for line and composition place his early decoys at the top of any collector's list. Of recent years, Lem has taken up the carving and painting of ornamental birds. They are highly decorative on the mantel or the coffee table, but are a far cry from the working decoys he made for use on the waters of the Chesapeake.

Not only did the styles and patterns of painting differ widely, the surface treatment and the brushwork included a variety of techniques: stippling, flecking, specking, scoring, scratch-coating, double brushwork, and use of the graining comb.

An effective impression of feathers could be evoked by wavy lines made with a comb. After the basecoat had dried, the darker top coat was applied. While this was still wet, a comb was literally combed through the darker coat to reveal the underlying off-white base. This graining technique has long been used by decorators of country furniture as well as decoy-makers.

When the collector tries to identify his decoy via the painting, he must remember that the hunters did not go by the book, and they took many liberties. Furthermore, they were in the habit of repainting season after season, and if the mallards had not been flying well but the blacks had, the mallard decoys were repainted to look like blacks. To determine the correct species it is wise to consider the conformation of the decoy as well as the color patterns—and then, to allow room for a great deal of imagination!

A number of the early decoys were not painted at all, but were treated with a wood preservative such as creosote, which darkens the wood, accents the graining, and creates an illusion of feathers. Scorching and burning in Indian fashion also sealed the pores of the wood without the necessity for paint. Sometimes a wax or tallow was melted into the undersurface as a protective coating. Pitch pine and cypress hold up fairly well in water without any special treatment.

George Marcus Winslow, of Duxbury, Massachusetts, carved an extraordinary set of yellowlegs about 1835. He created the feathering effect on his birds by a most frugal and ingenious method: He took a chisel, sharpened the edge, and walked it up and down the birds!

These unpainted birds, with their mellow wood tones acquired through the years, appeal strongly to people as well as to birds. Contemporary architecture and furnishings surround man with so many hard, glassy, synthetic surfaces that he longs for the old-fashioned comforts of the tree—its famili-

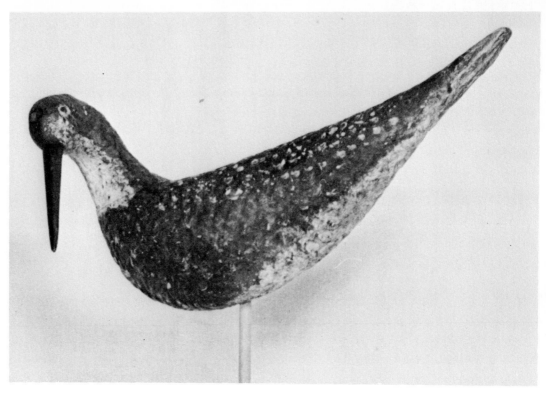

118. WINTER YELLOWLEGS

arity, its texture, and its warmth. Whatever the surface treatment of the decoy, whether painted or unpainted, whether chiseled or weathered, the final result had to be a soft finish. A shiny, reflecting surface—unnatural to a bird—scares away the wildfowl.

The Store-bought Decoy

In the 1880's, the manufactured decoy appeared on the market. Three companies are known to have developed a good business: the Mason Decoy Factory and the Dodge Decoy Factory, both in Detroit, Michigan; and the C. W. Stevens Factory at Weedsport, New York. All offered the public a general line of wooden lures. Their standard decoys—mostly ducks—sold for about fifty cents apiece.

It may seem odd to include a manufactured product in a book on folk arts, but the factory bird had a significant effect on the homemade decoy— both bad and good. The availability of a "boughten" object has the effect of discouraging the individual worker and his own self-expression, which is the basis of folk art as well as of all art. But the excellent taste shown by the better decoy companies did make itself felt in the work of the home carvers. The modeling and painting of the top-grade Mason decoys were so superior that they were copied happily by numberless baymen who had not been able to figure out as attractive and workable a decoy by themselves.

137

119. MAMMOTH CANVASBACK

The decoy companies also offered the advantage of employment to many skilled craftsmen in need of jobs. Handcraft was still a major part of manufacture in those days. The word "manufacture" did not mean what it does today—the work of a vast, faceless corporation that mechanically turns out its products. The meaning was closer to the Latin derivation—"a making by hand." The individual models were designed by the finest woodworkers to be found in the neighborhood. And after the duplicating lathe had reproduced the model, the finishing and painting were done by hand.

120. BROADBILL

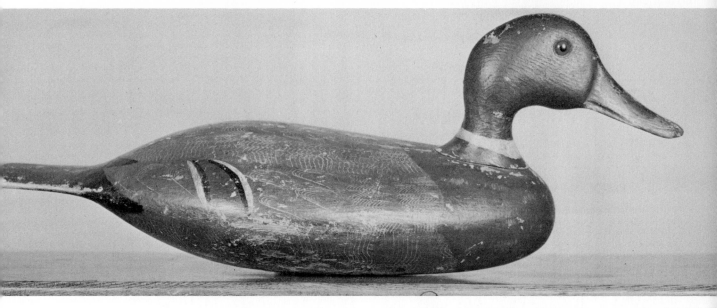

121. STEVENS FACTORY MALLARD DRAKE

The factories were not huge. They were simply places of work that employed some half-a-dozen men in a vacant shed or loft. And sometimes, the decoy "company" was a one-man operation, or a man and his wife.

The factory-produced weathervanes of this period—the moulded, hand-hammered copper horses, roosters, and fish that topped our barns and our meeting-houses—are considered part of the American folk art scene for the same reason that the best of the early factory decoys are. Both objects were well designed and practical; both helped to sustain the traditional crafts as well as the craftsmen at a time when growing industrialization and the development of new processes, materials, and inventions had forced many woodworkers into retirement.

The steamboat had outmoded the sailing ships that had carried on the maritime business of the world for centuries, and the newly powered ships had little use for the old hand-carved figureheads and sternboards, or for the men who carved them. The iron foundries cast not only pots, pans, and stoves but also cigarstore Indians and such toys as little horses, dolls, and wagons—objects once hand-carved from wood and today treasured in our museums.

Fortunately for everyone concerned, some of the displaced wood workers and pattern-makers were still available for the decoy factories. The Mason Decoy Factory hired the best. It is not known who they were—one may have been William Mason himself. Their catalogue boasted that "nothing has been spared to make these goods surpass anything in the shape of a decoy that heretofore has been manufactured." With even greater assurance, they stated flatly that they were "the largest exclusive manufacturer of decoys in the world." And I guess they were.

Though the Mason factory is listed in an 1899 Detroit directory, it is believed that they had been in business on a small scale for a number of years before that. During the approximately twenty-five years of their existence—they closed in 1914—they had shipped thousands of birds all over the United States. Specimens still turn up in the most obscure places as well as in the rigs of the better-known hunting camps. The better grades, in their original paint, are well worth searching for and have become valuable collector items.

Little is known about the history of the company itself. It is said to have started as a paint factory. The paint on the Mason decoy does stand up better and look better than that of any other commercial decoy, and over the years the surfaces have acquired a rich, satiny sheen.

Mason offered wooden lures for nearly every kind of wildfowl hunted: ducks, geese, shorebirds, and even swan and crows. The ducks were made of

122. "MASON" MALLARDS IN FOUR GRADES   A. PREMIER

B. CHALLENGE

C. STANDARD

D. FOURTH

cedar and priced in four grades: Premier, Challenge, Detroit (Standard), and Fourth—the mistakes. By lining up the different grades of one species it is easy to see what the less costly models lost in fullness and modeling. The lowest grade, dull and nondescript, lacks expression.

The Premier grades, however, are handsome, especially in the outsized models; they sold for twenty-one dollars a dozen. The look of the Mason duck is unmistakable—the strong, rolling sweep of the body, the poised head, and the typical scoop and crosscuts where the bill joins the head. The Premier

124.   REDHEAD: DRAKE (LATE)

123.   REDHEAD: DRAKE (EARLY)

is usually hollow, the others solid. Through the years, little change in styling took place, except that the later birds show somewhat less detail. The basic shapes of the various species are similar. For example, there is little differentiation between the green-wing teal and the blue-wing teal except for the paint pattern. The hen and the drake of the bluebill look alike except for their painting. Individuality is, of course, the one great quality sorely missing in the factory product.

Many gunners complain that the Mason duck decoys are too narrow, and roll in rough water. But if this is true, many hunters and many ducks were still fooled.

125. GREEN-WING TEAL: DRAKE
126. BLUE-WING TEAL: DRAKE

Mason shorebird decoys are prized even more highly than the ducks—and are rarer. Their curlew—Hudsonian or long-billed, and sickle-billed—are especially magnificent. The former was offered in two styles: a one-piece bird with the head withdrawn; and a bird in two sections, with the head high and erect.

However similar, the designs of all Mason shorebirds are simple and pleasing. As in the case of the ducks, many of the various patterns are so much alike that it is difficult to distinguish one bird from another except by its paint. If the paint is worn or weathered, it is almost impossible to tell a greater yellowlegs from a willet, or a lesser yellowlegs from a dowitcher.

127. "MASON" HUDSONIAN CURLEW

Birds with wood bills are of earlier vintage than those with iron bills. On all these birds, however, there is no detail of wing, tail, or head, because feather-cutting is difficult in lathe work.

A few companies supplied birds in tin and in iron as well as wood. One company, whose name is unknown, did a lively business selling tin snipe that were practically indestructible. Although the birds bear a patent date of 1874, many examples are still found in the hunting areas along the northern Atlantic coast. The supply house was probably in the East and may possibly have been H. H. Kiffe, 523 Broadway, New York City, which advertised tin snipe (plover and yellowlegs) for three dollars a dozen—no doubt the going rate.

These tin decoys are delightful and ingenious. Each is stamped in two half rounds that are wired together with tiny hinges at the head and tail. Laid open, these split snipe pack handily on top of one another, like saucers. They were sold in sets, packaged neatly in a wooden box, complete with dowel sticks for mounting. Each stick had a small brass collar that locked the halves of the bird together when it was closed and set on the beach.

Not all duck decoys floated. Iron ducks, for use on sink boxes in battery shooting, were cast by several local foundries situated around Chesapeake Bay. These extremely heavy decoys, weighing about thirty pounds each, also

128. "MASON" DOWITCHER AND DOVE

129. CAST-IRON BRANT

doubled as weights on the wings of the sink boxes, keeping the flanges flush
with the surface of the water and acting as stabilizers. The iron brant in
the illustration is a magnificent sculptural object, and a perfect example of
the unity of use and beauty that characterizes folk art.

Most of the early decoy companies closed shop after battery gunning
had been silenced by law and the sale of wildfowl prohibited. But a surprising number of lesser companies continued. Their names—among them,
Evans, Pratt, Burkhard, Pasaquala, Victor, and Tuveson—appear on the
underside of many a duck.

Today, the sporting companies provide useful decoys in a variety of
materials: plastic, latex, and papier-mâché, as well as wood. But these
products, entirely machine-made, have no relation to folk art.

Hudsonian Curlew in Surf

THE MEN WHO CARVED

THE MEN WHO CARVED

Most folk art, by its very nature, is anonymous, the work of people, not of names. The product counted, not the man. It is satisfying to look at a decoy and state with authority the name of the carver and the provenance, but this is difficult.

A very few eighteenth-century carvers and some of the nineteenth are identifiable, not because they made a name for themselves, but because some descendant or record exists. Usually, however, the unique style of the decoy itself serves as the author's signature.

The more recent carvers—those of the early twentieth century—are easier to identify, especially if they made decoys for hunting companions who extolled their capabilities and promoted their decoys among a small but enthusiastic circle of customers.

In describing these men and their work, I have made no attempt to compile a comprehensive catalogue. A complete list, in any case, would be next to impossible. Nor have I included the names of carvers just because they were "known." The fact that a man is known, perhaps because he sold widely, does not mean that his birds are worth being noted. The majority of decoyists produced dull, if efficient, tollers with no thought, conscious or unconscious, of artistic merit. The men chosen here were individualists with a marked creative talent.

For convenience, the carvers have been grouped chronologically. But date has little to do with style and craftsmanship. A primitive decoy may be early or it may be found in the bayous of Louisiana today. The most sophisticated carvings I know were made in the 1860's. Craftsmanship was superior a hundred years ago, but the urge for self-expression is timeless.

130. MALLARD DRAKE

The two eighteenth-century carvings in the illustrations are as dis-
similar as if they had been carved centuries apart. The mallard drake, which
belonged to the Almy family, of Dartmouth, Massachusetts, and dates between 1770 and 1780, is a carefully rendered decoy, fully modeled, and
feather-carved. The merganser from Long Island of about the same time is
a real primitive—a slab root-head—the work of R. Williams of Sheepshead
Bay. (His initials are cut into the base of the decoy.) But for all its simplicity, it has that old magic. Its presence recalls poignantly the elusive
beauty of this wild bird of the sea (105 and 130).

The most sophisticated carver of the nineteenth century was undoubtedly Lothrop T. Holmes, of Kingston, Massachusetts (1824–1899). Holmes's
merganser decoys are a legacy any man would be proud to leave. The sensitive modeling and brushwork of these birds resemble the exquisite rendering
of waterfowl on Chinese scrolls and china. But there is no record that
Holmes journeyed to the Orient or to Hong Kong on a Yankee clipper, or
that he came in contact with the professional art of any land, including his
own. It seems unbelievable that these birds could come from the hands of
an untutored seaman who lived out his life in a small but most pleasant
village near Plymouth Harbor. But art is not limited by geography, time,
or even education—and nobody knows this better than the folk art collector.

Unlike Holmes, Captain Osgood, of Salem, Massachusetts, was a seasoned voyager. According to legend, the Captain sailed west in 1849 and

131. AMERICAN MERGANSERS (HOLMES)

carved the Canada goose shown here "while waiting in a California port to return with his new cargo. When he came back to Massachusetts, he took the decoys up the Rowley River to a friend's hunting lodge, and they remained there until they were found a hundred years later."[9] Osgood's mergansers are as extraordinary as his geese and are characterized by the same flowing elegance.

It is odd that many of the fine early decoys from New England are mergansers (also called sheldrakes), considering that the flesh is notoriously rank and unpalatable. But the bird itself is so strikingly handsome, with its crest and glossy colors, that it seems to have had an inspiring effect on the carvers.

An extraordinary pair of American Mergansers is the hen and drake by Captain Ben Davis who lived on Monhegan Island, Maine. His birds are bold, strong, wide of beam, and seaworthy; their heads resemble a ship's prow. They remind me of the Viking ships that touched these same shores centuries ago.

132. CANADA GOOSE (OSGOOD)

Many shorebird decoys are known to have been made relatively early, but it is rare that one can place a bird, its carver, and its date together. The "winter" yellowlegs by George Marcus Winslow, of Duxbury, Massachusetts, can be dated about 1835. The dowitcher by William Henry Weston, of the same town, was carved in the 1860's. (Plates 118 & 36)

In contrast to the sophistication of the New England decoys by Holmes and Osgood, there are many handsome primitives from Long Island. One of these is the Labrador gull by Captain C.K. Ketchum of Copiague. The Captain's son Al said that his father used to float the gull off to one side of his brant rig as a "confidence" decoy, when he went hunting the brant goose along Great South Bay. Al presented the bird to Joel Barber, who had just begun to collect decoys and was the first fowler to consider the use of the decoy as a hunting art. Now that Mr. Barber's collection has been given to the Shelburne Museum, the gull—saved by the merest chance—will have an honored position in the history of American arts.

The black duck by Wilbur R. Corwin, who lived in the neighboring town of Bellport, is another unpainted primitive of the same period. Corwin's patterns are said to have been handed down in the family for generations, but few antique Corwin ducks are known to be extant.

Henry F. Osborne is the most controversial name among the nineteenth-century Bellport carvers. A few decoys are known to have come from his hand, but many shorebirds—yellowlegs, plover, and sandpipers—have been attributed to him with very little proof. All are of a similar type; they are charming, and deftly carved. The eye is a scribed circle, not glass or a tack. The wing curve is indicated in low relief, and where the tail feathers meet there is a pronounced and wide V. The tail itself shows a high ridge.

My attempts to trace these fine carvings lead me to guess that a number of men working in a similar style created this regional Long Island decoy. Certainly, the variations in patterns and tooling indicate the work habits of

133. LABRADOR GULL (KETCHUM)

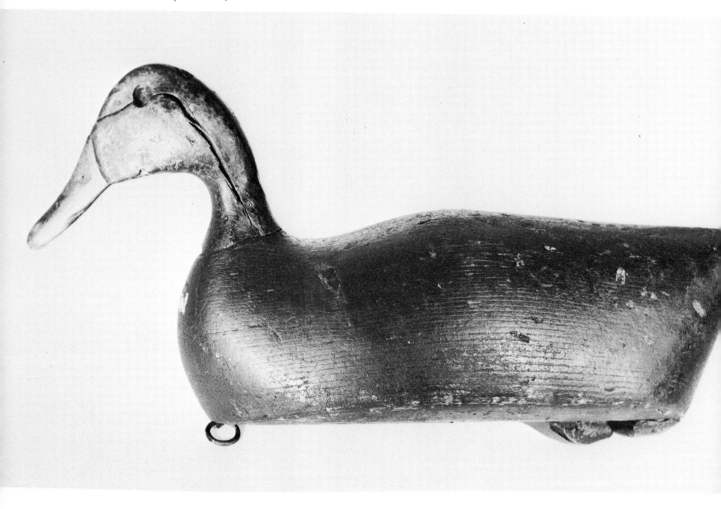

more than one man. Many carvers lived in the vicinity of Bellport and hunted along the same shore. Their names read like a cast of characters from an American frontier novel: Ben Hawkins, Caleb Carman, Daniel Havens, Rastus H. Post, and Obediah Verity.

My investigation of Osborne produced two interesting discoveries. Some years back, at an auction at the old Osborne place, several bushel baskets full of shorebird decoys were dragged out of the woodshed and the birds sold for fifty cents apiece. At least someone in the household made snipe decoys, and presumably it was "Henry F."

A more startling revelation came at the Shelburne Museum. While studying their collection, I found an "Osborne" yellowlegs that had the name "Laing" written on it. Albert Laing was the famous carver from Stratford, Connecticut. I was told that the little decoy had come to Shelburne in the Joel Barber collection and that "Cappy" Wicks, a Stratford gunner, had given it to Barber, telling him that Laing had carved it.

Today collectors agree generally that the so-called "Osborne" decoys were probably made by various members of the Verity family in Seaford, L.I. during the late 19th and early 20th centuries.

Albert Davids Laing (1811–1886) and Benjamin Holmes (1843–1912), renowned Connecticut carvers, lived along the Housatonic River and inspired a whole school of followers. Later, the decoyists of this region were to be known by the impressive title of the "Stratford School," with Charles E. Wheeler as their star. Both Laing and Holmes made wonderfully suave, curvaceous ducks, beautifully proportioned. The designs of the two men are similar, but Laing's birds are considered superior. This is as it should be for Laing was the older man and the chief creator of the unique "Stratford" decoy.

Laing must have been an interesting man to know. In 1863, he settled in Stratford, where he enjoyed the life of a gentleman sportsman, perfectionist, agriculturalist, and scholar. Being the son of a well-to-do Quaker merchant, he had leisure for the joys of wildfowling.

But the river decoys of that day, called "old rocking horses," displeased him. They were awkward to handle and clumsy to look at. He decided to make a better decoy, one more efficient and more pleasing: one that matched in quality the high grade of his English fowling pieces. He succeeded. Like most gentlemen of his station, he had all the necessary tools and skills, for he had been in the habit of making a great deal of his own sporting equipment, such as fishing rods, boxes, and sculling oars. According to Thomas C. Marshall, an eminent modern sportsman—to whom I am indebted for information concerning the Stratford decoy-makers—the Laing decoys were fashioned so expertly that they are as tight and good now as on the day they were finished.

Because he kept a "Farming and Shooting Record," Laing's activities and habits are known in some detail. He wrote pertinent statistics as well as natural observations, such as the dates when the ice went out, the striped bass first appeared, and the tree swallows left. By the summer of 1886, Laing had suffered a series of illnesses that left him in failing health. Being a perfectionist and impatient with infirmity, one October afternoon he shot himself. The last entry in his journal read, "Today, the martins left...."

After his death, the inventory of his estate included "one hundred and eleven stool ducks—$45." It was a modest item, but the one for which he will probably be remembered.

Benjamin Holmes, a completely different kind of man, was neither a sportsman nor a hunter. The decoys he made were strictly for sale—which may explain in part why his ducks are not as durable as Laing's. But Holmes was a finish carpenter by trade, he had an excellent eye, and the basic Stratford design had already been developed by Laing. Holmes won a prize at the Philadelphia Exposition in 1876 with twelve broadbills.

The majority of Holmes's decoys are blacks, whistlers, and broadbills. There is little difference in the poses, and there is no record that he made any "sleepers"; Laing created birds in a wide variety of attitudes and head positions. Some of Laing's birds were alert, with high heads; some were at rest, with low heads snuggled in a puffed-up, sleepy position. Strange to say, all of Laing's ducks have blunt tails; he did not distinguish between the tails of the "dabblers" and those of the divers. Although Laing made only drakes for his shooting rig, Holmes was more broadminded—he made both hens and drakes.

Another credit must go to Laing for the painting of the decoys; he originated the Stratford style of brushwork as well as the sculptural conformation. It has been rumored that Holmes did no painting of his decoys at all but turned this task over to Robert Plumb.

Laing's exact method of painting can only be guessed, but the pattern he set for the black duck has been followed by generations of Stratford carvers. The body was painted with flat black, which had been lightened to a dark brown with a little burnt umber. There was no wing patch. The head was painted the same color as the body, but after the several basecoats had dried, a buff color of burnt umber and white was brushed on head and neck, with the exception of the crown and the eye streak. While this last coat was still wet, a sharpened stick was used to cut irregular lines through the paint so that the dark of the undercoat would show through.

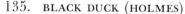

135. BLACK DUCK (HOLMES)

136. WHISTLER (HOLMES)

137. BROADBILL (HOLMES)

How does one tell a Laing from a Holmes? This is not easy—unless you happen to be Thomas C. Marshall. The most important difference can be seen by looking down at the decoy from above. The body shape of a Laing is oval, with the stern almost as full as the breast; the body of a Holmes, on the other hand, is almost pear-shaped, with the narrow end at the breast. Also, the breast has more overhang, and the side of the body joins the bottom without the rounding that characterizes the Laing duck.

Boatmen would say that the Holmes decoy has a sharper chine than the Laing. Also, the body of the Holmes is higher, the most prominent part being about three-quarters of the way back from the breast, whereas the highest part of the Laing decoy is about center. These differences are easily seen in the accompanying photographs.

A Laing signature is, of course, certain identification, but only a few had the regular branded "LAING." Some have the name F. BURRITT on the bottom. Commodore Francis Burritt was not a maker, though—he was a local sportsman.

138. PINTAIL (LAING)

To the collector, it is important not only to distinguish between a Laing and a Holmes, but to be able to tell copies from originals. A number of local carvers copied the models, not to deceive future collectors, but simply to take advantage of a good workable design in making their own hunting rigs. Their work was expedited by the availability of the actual patterns. For example, R. I. Culver bought the Holmes patterns and made a set. William Baldwin borrowed the Culver patterns, and many contemporary carvers copy the Baldwins. It was also quite simple for a good woodworker to borrow an original Laing or Holmes and duplicate it. Some even tried to improve it. The results are bastards that have confused many collectors and many museums.

To help in identifying a "Laing," I have included a series of photographic studies of one of his decoys, a sleeping canvasback made about 1863. The decoy has been repainted, but I know of no "Laing" that still has its original coat. The eleven close-ups of this fine decoy clearly reveal the characteristics of Laing, as well as his feeling for sculptural form.

139.   STUDIES OF A CANVASBACK

139A.

139B.

139C.

139D.

139E.

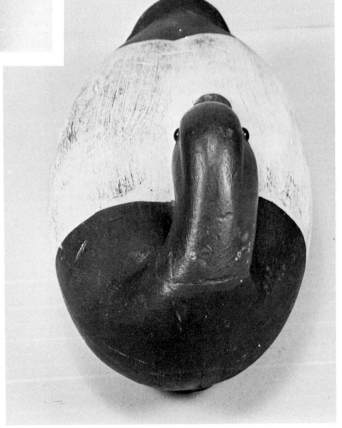

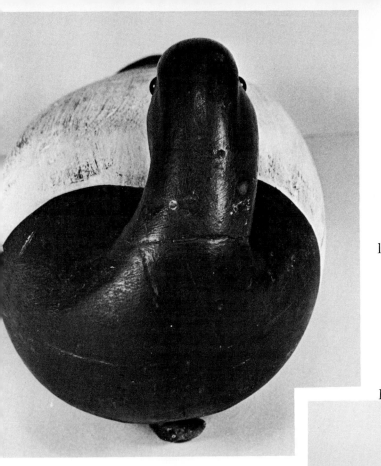

139f.

139g.

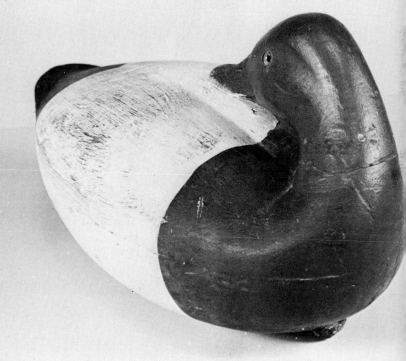

139h.

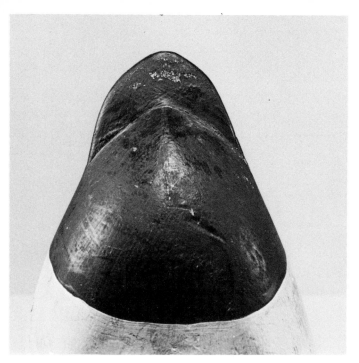

139ɪ.

139ɪ.

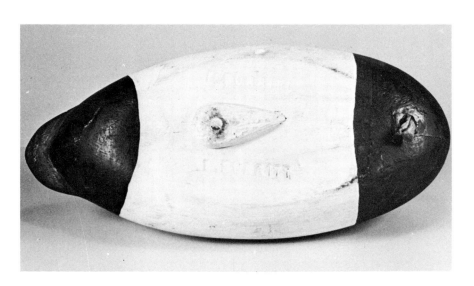

139ᴋ.

Most of the recognized carvers from the New Jersey and the Delaware areas worked mainly in the early years of the twentieth century. The few whose work does belong in the nineteenth century include Gideon Lippincott, Charlie Parker, Henry Grant, Cooper Predmore, Winfield White, Dan English, and John Blair.

Blair, who lived in Philadelphia and shot over the marshes of the Delaware, made exceptionally intriguing decoys, which look completely modern. The painting is said to have been done by another, a professional. Whether this statement is true or false, the painting matches the distinctive grace and simplicity of the carving.

140. PINTAIL (BLAIR)

Nineteenth-century decoys from the shores of Virginia and the Carolinas are rather blocky and undistinguished, with the exception of those made by the Cobb family, of Cobb's Island, Virginia. The eminent collector William J. Mackey, Jr., reports:

> The island was named for Nathan F. Cobb, who had bought it for a hundred dollars in 1838, a year after his sloop was driven ashore on a nearby coast while he was taking his family south in search of a climate less hard on his ailing wife than that of their native Massachusetts. Nathan had many children, who matured and prospered as merchants, fishermen, oystermen, salvage experts, hunting and fishing guides . . .[10]

141. SHOREBIRD DECOYS: CURLEW, PLOVER, AND ROBIN SNIPE

Cobb's eldest boy, Nathan, Jr., was the chief of the decoy carvers. His N, with its distinctive serifs, is usually carved into the underbody of his birds. His brother Elkenah signed with an E, and Arthur with an A.

All the Cobb decoys bear a family resemblance. They are chunky, with great depth in the body. The brant geese are said to have been hewn from ship masts that washed up on the beach. Although little detail is evident, one distinctive feature marks all Cobb decoys: the blunt separation of the wing tips from the tail. For all their bulky appearance, these birds have the authoritative look that comes from a knowledge of the birds and a sure hand on the chisel.

Many twentieth-century carvers are known by name. Those chosen to represent this period are men who continued to work in the old traditions but who also developed a personal style—men whose work has historical and esthetic significance.

Historically, Joel Barber (1877–1952), of Wilton, Connecticut, contributed more to the awakening of interest in decoys than any other single man. He started to collect in the 1920's, and his early recognition of the decoy as a work of art saved many of our best examples from oblivion. His book *Wild Fowl Decoys,* written in 1934, gave the decoy a dignified status in the annals of American wildfowling. He himself carved few birds. He was an architect by profession and chiefly interested in design and construction. He always dreamed that one day he might create the perfect decoy.

Barber's collection first attracted notice in the historic Bellport Decoy Show of 1923, an event sponsored by the local Anti-Duskers' Society. ("Dusking" is the ignominious practice of shooting birds as they come in to feed after dark.) The Bellport Show was the first known decoy exhibition, and it was a great success. It brought to light fine examples of nineteenth-century decoys and stimulated competition among contemporary carvers. The show must have been stunning. It included superlative examples of birds by Joel Barber, Charles E. Wheeler, A. E. Crowell, Wilbur R. Corwin, and Henry F. Osborne. Unfortunately, there is no photographic record.

Today, this Long Island area, which includes Moriches Bay and Shinnecock as well as Great South Bay, still breeds a group of passionate fowlers as dedicated to hunting the decoy as the duck. In the last forty years, since that first Bellport show, many excellent regional carvers have been tracked down, including Thomas Gelston, Frank Kellum, Lester Gardner, P. W. Bigelow, Gil Smith, George Havens, and Charles Strang.

Unquestionably, the most famous name among all decoy-carvers is Anthony Elmer Crowell (1862–1951), of East Harwich, Massachusetts. *The Boston Sunday Globe,* on September 20, 1914, stated flatly that connoisseurs recognized Crowell's birds as "the best decoys produced by hand in any workshop."

This claim may have been inspired by enthusiasm for a native son. But it is true that Crowell's shorebirds are recognized as the "best" of any known carver. His ducks and geese vary in quality from the superb to the common. And he was the first to say so.

Crowell was an outspoken gentleman with the ingenuous wit typical of a Cape Codder. Many Harwich residents still remember Elmer vividly. He was a round, ruddy-faced man with twinkling blue eyes, who loved to sit with his hands folded across his plump stomach, telling tales of the time when he was young, skinny, and a crack shot.

142. PORTRAIT OF A. ELMER CROWELL

Gunning was the passion of his life, much to the consternation of his father, who was a proper fisherman and cranberry grower, and disliked all weapons. Regardless of his father's disapproval, Elmer owned a gun by the time he was twelve—a breachloader, the first on the Cape. Having acquired a gun, he built a duck blind on Long Pond, now called Pleasant Lake. On his first "shoot," he and his tame drake, which he used as a live decoy, called in four ducks—and he got one.

Many flavorful details of his life are known because of an article written by a friend and neighbor, Dorothea Setzer, and published in the *Cape Cod Compass* in 1951. It is worth quoting at length.

He started to make decoys when he was only ten; at fourteen he carved out Black duck and Whistler life-size models, but none were sold until 1898. In his early youth, Crowell found out that when he left his "coys" on the water for future use, often on his return

143.   CROWELL IN FRONT OF WORKSHOP

144.   WORKSHOP OF A. ELMER CROWELL

some would have disappeared, and others been mutilated. He decided that something must be done about this, so he hit upon the idea of fashioning removable heads. Thus when his sport was over for the day, he calmly put the heads in his pockets and left only a useless block of wood behind!

Dr. John C. Phillips, who bought his first decoys, hired Crowell to take charge of his camp at Wenham Lake, and develop it. While here he acted as guide for nine Harvard students, who subsequently became his best customers. He whiled away his evening hours whittling little ducks, using shavings for the wings, and pinning them up on the ceiling. Martha Phillips, then in her early teens, rode by with two little foreign friends, dismounted to watch the drake catch the corn being fed him, and caught sight of the mural decoration. The youngsters begged the little birds from the good-natured guide, and took five.

As a result, some months later orders came from France for more of these small models then unpainted and marked only with lead pencil. Thus encouraged, young Crowell whittled assiduously, making only ducks, but improving his work by painting his subjects. In his middle teens he had prevailed upon his parents to allow him to take twenty-four painting lessons from Miss Emily King of Middleboro, who spent her summers at Harwich Port and taught at $1.00 per lesson; this was the only professional instruction he ever had.[11]

The following excerpts about the carving of miniatures and song birds rather than working decoys are included because they throw light on all of Crowell's work:

In 1908 two women whose names escape Mr. Crowell's memory, came from Osterville, wanting song birds. They succeeded in overcoming his modest, but vigorous, protests, and he complied by making a chipping sparrow; it must have been good for it brought more orders. It was a natural sequence, having fashioned ducks and song birds, to try his hand at shorebirds, the first of which was bought by Dr. Cunningham of Brookline. In these early days the birds were mounted on flat, square, black bases, and originally tacks were used for the eyes, and painted, but later, eyes were imported from England. Subsequently he put his models on mounts that conformed to their habits; he carved and painted sea and fresh water clam shells, quahaug and scallop shells, and rocks, so realistically that one can scarcely believe that they are not the genuine article. . . .

Mr. Crowell always drew his birds first, and made his own patterns, but it was some years before he became expert enough to sketch his birds to scale when he made them other than life size. All birds received two prime coats of paint in thin colors, and the markings were applied a minimum of four to five times. White cedar is used exclusively, which must be cut in winter when the sap is dry, and this is seasoned, under cover, for three and four years. If the wood is cut in warm weather the sap stays up and it cannot be carved.

Crowell once paid a neighbor $5.00 for two fine, clean cedar stumps, about 30 inches in diameter; his friend thought him a bit daft to buy enough cedar for what he felt would take a life-time of whittling, but these stumps, used only for miniatures, were worked up in about six months' time! . . .
In the humble little wooden shed in East Harwich where these small masterpieces are turned out, one could always find a child's copy book, with pencil attached. After discussing one's wishes with the Master one was told to write down name, address, type of bird wanted, and the date on which it had been promised—should it have been requested for a special occasion. Thus all orders were filled in the order of receipt, or promise, and in the true independent, democratic Cape Cod spirit, no advantages were accorded anyone!

On three separate occasions he refused financial backing to make his birds on a wholesale scale. The idea appalled him, and he felt that without the individual touch his work would be without merit. He has never regretted his decision, and seriously doubts that, as the manager of a commercial enterprise, he would be better off financially today, than he is as a superlatively successful craftsman.[11]

The Crowell touch is always unmistakable, although his styles of carving and painting varied, as might be expected, through the fifty-odd years of his work. The early ducks were sturdy, simplified forms with little detail, but they were obviously good "callers." In his late years, the ducks did become more detailed, and even ornate—something that often happens when a good craftsman grows older. With more time for sitting and less for the active life, Crowell became intrigued by his own dexterity and began to carve and paint minute differentiations. He also discovered that the highly decorated birds, destined for the mantel rather than the marsh, brought a better price. A pretty yellowlegs standing on a wooden quahaug shell sold for twenty-five dollars, but a plain, hardworking duck decoy brought only five dollars, or at most, ten.

The best duck decoys come from the middle period in Crowell's life, when his craft was fully developed and before his love of detail for detail's sake made his art mannered. In the ideal Crowell decoy both the carving and the painting *accent* the essential shape instead of breaking it up.

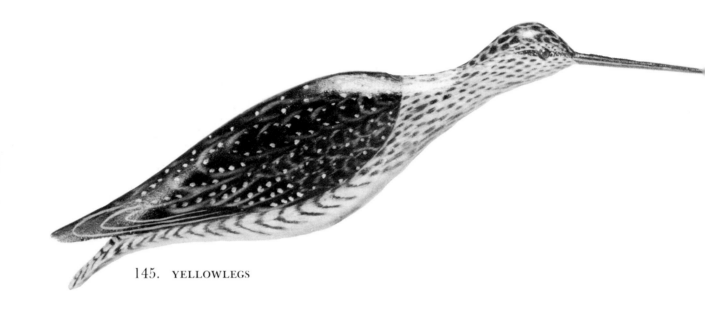

145. YELLOWLEGS

146. CROWELL SEAGULLS IN SILHOUETTE

147. CROWELL DECOYS: BLACK-BREASTED PLOVER,
YELLOWLEGS, AND EARLY BLACK DUCK

Crowell admittedly made birds of varying quality and sold them as such, to suit the needs and the pocketbook of his customer. Certain orders were for gunners who wanted the decoys to shoot over for a couple of seasons, after which they could be thrown away. These tollers have little modeling of head and neck and no distinctive feather-carving or painting. They are ordinary, and not even the magic of the Crowell name has the power to enhance them. But great numbers, literally hundreds, were shaped with care, were marked by the sensitive and sure hand of the master, and most of these were also thrown away.

Crowell's reputation rests firmly on his shorebirds. They are without peer, as distinguished as the famous Audubon prints—as natural and as lovingly interpreted. Crowell was a devoted ornithologist, and the poses and the painting of a number of his decoys reflect the Audubon influence.

The most sculptural examples of his shorebird decoys, those modeled with full wing contours and full breast, are probably early, from the 1900 to 1910 period. The more simplified versions, in which the wings are defined not by modeling but by a low-relief cut or a painted line, are somewhat later, made during a period when he was developing a more streamlined form that was easier to turn out. The pair of "beetleheads" (black-breasted plovers) illustrated (34) is known to have been made to order about 1915.

148. BLACK DUCK

149. REDHEAD

150. CURLEWS AND MINIATURES

In 1918 shorebird gunning was outlawed, and that meant the end of snipe-carving. In the photograph of Crowell, the birds on his workbench are not decoys, but what he called "ornamentals." It is interesting to see that the ornamental curlew in the picture has a style similar to that of his working curlew decoy.

Crowell's painting also helps to set the chronology of his birds. In the first years, he used only a few plain colors: black, white, and umber. By mixing these three in varying proportions, he arrived at his brownish hues. This does not mean that his early painting lacked distinction. On the contrary, it is rich with subtle variations in brush stroke, tone, and density. He preferred a dry brush, so that the areas of paint were controlled. The bristles were not loaded with paint and remained dry enough to simulate the individual feather lines.

173

Later, about 1910, he added more colors to his palette. Instead of relying on simple tonal values for his effects, he used four or five different colors and built them up with a variety of brush techniques. He dabbed with a full brush, and this produced a pebbly surface. He stippled and dotted. And he drew both soft and hard finish-lines to accent the edge of the plumage. These processes can be seen clearly in the painting of his yellow-legs.

Whichever techniques he used, the plumage achieved a unique feeling of soft, deep feathers—an effect for which he is justly famous. His birds probably look better now than when he first painted them. Age and weather often enhance the beauty of painted wood surfaces. Fading produces color tones not found in a paintbox. Blacks become soft rusts and blue-grays, and white mellows. In places where the paint was thinly applied, wear begins to reveal the warm tones of the wood underneath.

Crowell earned such respect as a painter that a number of decoy-carvers of inferior talents hired him to dress up their birds. Keyes Chadwick of Martha's Vineyard is said to have shipped his unpainted birds to Crowell by the bushel basket.

In trying to identify a Crowell shorebird decoy, it is helpful to become acquainted with two special characteristics of his work: the typical separation of wing tips from the tail, and the dark brushmark through the eyes.

The most satisfying identification is the Crowell stamp on the base. Birds from the 1898 to 1900 years are reported to carry a square stamp, although I have never seen one. The oval stamp, dating from 1900, bears the legend:

A. ELMER CROWELL

DECOYS. EAST HARWICH

MASS.

After Elmer Crowell's death in 1951, his son Cleon, who had often worked at his father's side, continued to carve birds, mostly miniatures, and used his father's patterns and stamp. But after two years he stopped this practice, for he realized the confusion it was causing. Cleon died in 1961. But his widow still cherishes Elmer's old, original patterns and guards them zealously. They might tempt some ambitious craftsman to make reproductions, because Crowell's birds—whether decoys, miniatures, or ornamentals—are few and passionately hunted.

The whole Cape Cod region, which was a wildfowl paradise in the old days, produced many fine carvings, but the majority are anonymous. Three known decoyists lived on the island of Martha's Vineyard: Henry Keyes

Chadwick, Ben Smith, and Frank Adams. All were woodworkers by trade, and their birds are clean, solid, and practical.

Chadwick (1868–1959) was the first of the island carvers. In his lifetime he must have made between seven and eight hundred decoys—mostly blue-bills, redheads, and widgeons—but few have survived the years. Many of them, incidentally, are branded with "Foote." Captain Robert Foote, of West Tisbury, was his best customer.

151. OLD SQUAW: HEN

152. OLD SQUAW: DRAKE

153. BLACK DUCKS OF STRATFORD SCHOOL

On the mainland, at Accord, Massachusetts, lived a well-known and distinguished carver, Joseph Whiting Lincoln (1859–1938). The Lincoln ducks and geese have real style and beauty. The heads are regal, the bodies high and deep. I have never seen any of Lincoln's shorebirds, although two neighbors of his, Russ Burr and Chester Spear, are supposed to have followed his shorebird patterns. Mrs. Lincoln recalls that her husband did make shorebirds. She also speaks fondly of Joel Barber, who used to visit and admire their dahlias as well as their decoys. Barber tried to persuade Lincoln to make root-head decoys, Long Island style. He had no success.

Another contemporary of Crowell's was Charles E. ("Shang") Wheeler (1872–1949), of Westport and Stratford, Connecticut. The two men probably knew each other, but there is no record that they did. Certainly, Crowell's style had no effect on Wheeler. His birds were modeled after those of Laing and Holmes, and today he is considered the star of the Stratford school.

"Shang" was born into a well-to-do family, but he was a maverick and left home early to earn his own way and follow the sea. When he was not shipping on some sailing vessel, he liked to gun on the meadows and bays all along the Atlantic coast. He even tried market gunning as a way of making a living.

He started making his own decoys when he was still in his teens, simply because he could not afford to buy them. Since his home base was Stratford, it can be assumed that he knew Holmes, and we know that he was familiar with Laing's decoys, even though Laing died while Shang was still a boy. In any case, he followed the designs of the local decoys. For example, to make the body he joined two white-pine boards, each two inches thick, one on top of the other. This brought the seam above the waterline. Outsized tollers required heavier material, and in later years he occasionally joined a very thick board to a thin bottom plank.

Both the body and the head were shaped from patterns that outlined the top and side views. The roughing was done with a saw; and the details of bill tip, nostrils, cheeks, and the joining of head with bill were carved with a jackknife. True to the local tradition, the birds were hollow, flat-bottomed, and rigged with the body weight aft, so as to raise the full breast for better clearance in a fast current and in slush ice.

All of Wheeler's birds are well made and finished with the fine, flowing lines and balance that typify the Stratford group. The only part of a Wheeler decoy that shows any sign of sharpness is the middle of the stern, under the tail, where the sides join in an acute angle—a design similar to Laing's.

Wheeler made some decoys to shoot over, and others, quite similar, for exhibition. He loved to carve and paint. Although he liked to gun over his decoys, or just watch them bob in the water, he was never happier than when he was whittling or painting a new bird. He made three "settings" of

154. MALLARDS: DRAKE AND HEN

nearly every kind of wildfowl in North America, and usually three examples of each species: a male, a female, and a "sleeper."

One of these settings, containing almost every kind of wildfowl, forms an impressive display at the Birdcraft Museum in Fairfield, Connecticut. His one and only sandhill crane—a majestic bird—is a highlight of the Abby Aldrich Rockefeller Collection of Folk Art in Williamsburg, Virginia. The pair of Wheeler mallards that won the grand championship at the Bellport Decoy Show in 1923 is a proud possession of the Shelburne Museum.

Although he enjoyed having his decoys admired at sportsmen's shows, he never guessed that one day his birds would find their way, as folk art, into museums. Regardless of the accolades he received, he had no commercial interest in making decoys. He never sold any—he gave them away. If someone he liked admired a decoy, he handed it over. "Take it," he'd say, "it's yours." Sometimes, he traded birds for books, or a boat, or a curly-haired retriever.

Aside from the wood decoys, he also made birds with cork bodies and wooden heads and tails. The bodies do not have the modeling or the fine painting of the wooden decoys, but they still show the Wheeler instinct for the pleasing proportion and the finely wrought head.

Wheeler worked from nature. He loved to watch the ducks in the local ponds and estuaries, especially when they were relaxing and resting. He studied their attitudes and, in particular, their head positions. Then, he would go home and try to catch their gracious, fluid shapes in his manmade birds. He was a realist with a sure instinct for sculptural form.

In his later years, he became interested in community and state affairs. As a state senator in the Connecticut legislature, he effectively voiced his views on conservation—of birds, fish and game, trees, and oysters. He was a large, handsome man with a full moustache, and when he spoke people listened. This made him a successful politician, a career aided by his very real talent as a cartoonist.

As a person, he is remembered chiefly for his extravagant generosity. When he was not giving away decoys or money, he was giving advice on how to make decoys, or tie a trout fly, or design a duckboat. He would give you almost anything—if he liked you. If he didn't, you didn't exist.

And he gave us the quiet pleasure of his lovely birds. His decoys are copied by a number of contemporary carvers—and copied well. True to form, he gave R. E. Bliss, a fellow gunner, some of his painting and carving patterns, just to help him out. Bliss's Canada goose, pintail, widgeon and white-winged scoter are difficult to distinguish from genuine Wheelers. One small difference is in the weights. Wheeler used an oval lead; Bliss's was pear-shaped. It is no sin to copy—copying is one way to learn. But it would be helpful if copies were signed by their makers.

155. THREE BLACK DUCKS

Many decoy carvers of the first years of this century on Long Island and New Jersey became known because of a growing interest in local history and in American wildfowling. As times changed, and better roads, power boats and gas-fired buggies cut down travel distance between hunting grounds and hunters, decoys were more easily exchanged, bought, and sold-and more readily copied.

Still a few decoyists kept their sense of individuality. Joseph Dawson of Trenton, New Jersey was a genuine artist; his ducks have a rare, sleek, and sophisticated style all their own. Dawson's favorite hunting grounds on Duck Island, in the Delaware, had also been a favorite haunt of Alexander Wilson, the ornithologist, a hundred years before.

Another fine painter was called "Jesse Birdsall" because that was the name of a man who once lived in the house at Barnegat where many of these beautiful decoys with their distinctive markings and tonal blend were found. Today it has been established that the most "Birdsall" decoys were made by John Dilley of Quogue, Long Island. (plate 156)

The one New Jersey carver who developed a solid reputation in his own **day** was Henry Van Nuckson Shourdes of Tuckerton. (1871 - 1920). Decoy-**carv**ing became his trade, and he made some ten thousand birds in his lifetime, shipping them everywhere from Maine to California. But his productivity failed to make him a rich man. He sold his birds for about fifty cents apiece. Today one of his shorebirds in original condition can command a price of two thousand dollars.

156. KNOT, RUDDY TURNSTONE, AND PLOVER

157. WHISTLER

158. CANVASBACKS

Shourdes developed a personal style, although he was really a one-man factory. His decoys—made from a simple pattern that was easy to duplicate—were neat, simple, and pleasing. His ducks and geese are clean-cut, with fine heads accented by a high forehead, fat cheeks, and a distinct shadow depression on the sides of the head. His yellowlegs, plover, and dowitchers are charming figures, but he made little differentiation in the size and contour of these species.

In the general region of Little Egg Harbor Bay and Barnegat Bay there were many known and respected families, like the Parkers, the Grants, the Gales, and the Ridgeways, who provided guides and decoys for the out-of-town hunters. The Shourdes workshop became a favorite gathering place for local and visiting fowlers, many of whom undoubtedly carved decoys in the Shourdes manner. It is said that the Tuckerton shop made decoys for the Cobbs of Virginia when that family of carvers preferred to do something else—like go fishing.

South from Barnegat and the Delaware, there is another mecca for decoy enthusiasts—Chrisfield, Maryland, on Chesapeake Bay. Its star, Lem Ward, shines brightly. He is very much alive and still carving.

159. CANADA GOOSE

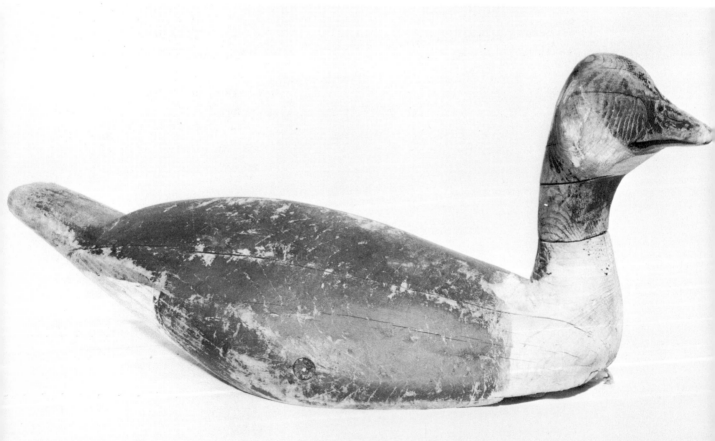

Lem and his brother Steve have gunned and whittled ever since they can remember, and they have sold thousands of decoys, although they have earned their living mainly as barbers. Steve is the practical member of the family, the one who takes care of the details of everyday living. Lem is recognized as the "artist," though he never saw the inside of an art school. On the contrary, he has figured out all the answers by himself, and his birds show a sense of form and have a vitality and grace that a professional would be proud of.

The Ward decoys are all ducks and geese; there are no shorebirds. The initial shaping of the body was done with a hatchet instead of the saw and drawknife used by such masters as Crowell and Wheeler. This gave their decoys bold, sure planes and a primitive vigor—qualities especially evident in the early decoys, such as the superb Canada goose illustrated here.

Lem's early bluebills have strong, sculptural, roly-poly shapes topped by vigorous heads. The pintail was also a favorite. He liked a low neck line that accented the high swell of the body and the clean rise of the head. The heads of the birds are a joy in themselves. Lem was very conscious of the relationship of contours—the soft curve of the crown as it played against the thrust of the beak. He has always experimented in poses and attitudes, trying to catch the quiet alertness of the wild duck.

His painting is admired as much as his carving. The methods have varied through the years, but he has been continuously aware of the three elements of good painting: color, pattern, and texture. His palette reflects the colors of the sea, the marsh grasses and their shadows, as well as the plumage itself. To obtain the typical pebbly effect of his surfaces, he first stipples with thick, white lead and a stiff brush. When this coat is dry, he brushes brown and black paint over it, wipes it off, and blends the colors.

After World War II, the style of the Ward decoys changed. As men returned from service, there was a sudden rush of orders, and the brothers looked for a material that was easier to work than the cedar, pine, and juniper they had always used. They discovered balsa and purchased surplus Navy life rafts in quantity. Balsa is buoyant, light in weight, and adaptable, but its lack of structural strength results in a weakness of structural form, and its texture has neither character nor color.

In very recent years, Lem has preferred to fashion ornamental and realistic birds instead of useful, working decoys. But he is becoming aware that the decoys he made in the 1920's and 1930's have a special importance in the field of folk arts, and he is quietly trying to buy some back. Decoys similar to Lem's and made in the same period by his friends Noah Sterling and Lloyd Tyler are also very much prized by collectors.

160. BLUEBILLS: EARLY AND LATE MODELS

161. HEAD OF EARLY "WARD" BLUEBILL

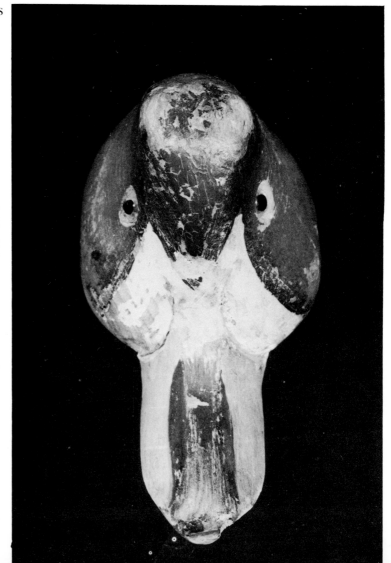

184

162. PINTAILS: HEN AND DRAKE

A few miles south of Chrisfield, as the duck flies, the Virginia shore
begins. Among the decoyists who lived here, two men stand out: Ira Hudson
(1877–1949), of Chincoteague, and Lee Dudley (1860–1942), of Knott's Island.
Dudley's ruddy ducks, usually signed LD, are the best of their kind, and
everything a ruddy duck should be—gay, fat, and saucy. In the 1930's, they
could be bought for five cents apiece. Today, their value has risen some
1,000 percent, and, as many a collector has discovered, they are not only rare,
they are virtually nonexistent.

In the Middle West, three outstanding decoy-carvers lived in Illinois,
a state that prides itself on being the best duck-hunting territory along the
Mississippi flyway. Here, Robert A. Elliston, Charles H. Perdew, and Bert
Graves built a reputation for themselves and set the patterns for the whole
area.

Elliston (1849–1915) is the granddaddy of all Illinois decoy-carvers. He
grew up near Indianapolis, and at the age of eighteen went to work in the
Studebaker shop as a maker of buggy and carriage bodies. Later, he improved
his status by taking a position in the factory of Henry Olds, and after moving

185

163. RUDDY

164. CANVASBACK

165. CANVASBACK

about for several years, following his trade, he settled at Lake Senachwine on the Illinois River. Here, he made his first decoys. In 1889, he moved to a town called Bureau and bought an apiary. He lived there happily ever after, raising bees and making decoys. His wife, Catherine, helped him in the painting of the decoys, and he was proudest of those they made together.

Charlie Perdew (1874–1963) helped Elliston in his shop, but he had made his first decoy alone. When he was fourteen, "he took the side rails of an old rope bed, cut them up in pieces and threw them in a fire to char. He then retrieved them, took a draw knife and cut some of the charring away to make bluebill decoys. These he used in Sawmill Lake about a mile from his home. Here he shot ducks for the Chicago market . . ." With each shipment of game, he included a free package of wild rice to promote sales. The rice grew in such abundance at the lake that he could gather it by pushing the boat through the rice and shaking the stalks over it. This spirit of enterprise, plus a healthy curiosity, characterized his whole life. He tried practically every trade that grew up in those booming years in the Middle West. Donald Clark records his life in these terms:

In 1889 Charlie went to Chicago . . . [where] he worked for a meat packing plant and as a carpenter 'to help put together' the Chicago World's Fair of 1893. At the same time, he attended the Chicago Art Institute to study painting. He left in 1893 and returned to Henry [Illinois]. Between the years 1893–1898 he did carpenter work in Henry, punched cattle in Kansas and operated a shooting gallery for the Peters Cartridge Company.

In 1898 back in Henry he started a bicycle livery and repair shop. In conjunction with this he made gun sales and repair. He began making boats which he continued to do through the years and he also began making crow decoys. . . .

During World War I due to lack of demand for hunting equipment he turned to the broom business. He grew his own broomcorn, built a machine to separate the seed from the straw and made brooms for which he received 40–75 cents apiece.

After the war he returned to decoymaking. In 1924 Charlie entered a pair of handmade mallard decoys in a decoy contest at Abercrombie & Fitch of New York and won second place for his craftsmanship.[12]

Perdew's wife, Edna, helped in the painting of the decoys until 1941, when illness prevented her from working further. It was her practice to "comb" the paint, whereas her husband obtained his effects with a stiff brush. Edna's decoys always had a slight edge over Charlie's, but he never seemed to mind.

166. MALLARD HEN

167. CROW AND TEAL

The most popular canvasback decoy in use on the Illinois River was one made by Bert Graves. It is a "high-head" and is still shot over along the river today.

The decoys of all three of these men are similar. They are composed of two pieces, hollowed out and joined; the bottoms are usually semirounded. Elliston and Graves both carved chunky heads with eyes set high, but Elliston carved the bill in greater detail, and Graves's tails are set higher than Elliston's. Perdew made slimmer heads, favored the sunken eye-socket, and usually carved a wing separation on the bodies. Most of these decoys carry the name of the maker, which is moulded into the long narrow lead weight screwed to the base of the decoy.

In the north, where Lake Ontario and the St. Lawrence River border New York State, lived another notable group of decoy-makers—ably represented by Frank Coombs and James E. Stanley.

Coombs was a typical river guide. When he was not hunting, he was a part-time barber and an employee of the local hotel. After he shot off half his right hand in a duck-blind accident, he had to give up his town job. But he did not let the accident interfere with his boat-building or decoy-carving, and thereafter spent most of his time guiding and hunting.

Coombs originated the distinctive and serviceable "Alexandria longneck" decoy, which carried its head high above the freezing water and prevented icing of the bill. His decoys have one eccentricity: He painted the feathers going in the wrong direction. The convex tips point to the bow rather than the stern.

The most noted guide in the Cape Vincent area was James E. Stanley (1856–1927). Sailor, adventurer, craftsman, naturalist—his life reads like the romantic dream of every schoolboy . . . that is, every schoolboy of a couple of generations ago.

Stanley was born in Sydney, Australia. When he was only twelve, he decided to become a sailor, and when of age, he joined a "school ship" in the British Navy. After his term of duty expired, he shipped on sailing vessels, touching practically every port on the seven seas. On two occasions he spent six months in Greenland hunting whales and seals. Once, when his vessel was wrecked off a deserted island in the Caribbean, he was given up as lost at sea.

During his wanderings, Stanley developed a keen interest in the native birdlife of the lands he visited, and on several occasions he collected rare specimens for the British Museum. He was even commissioned to journey down the Amazon River into the wilderness of South America to gather exotic birds for a Florida collector.

These assignments made it necessary for him to learn the skills of taxidermy, and he enjoyed building habitat groups of birdlife. A number of these have been used by the Museum of Natural History in New York City. When he finally settled down at Cape Vincent, his own home took on the appearance of a small museum, filled with cases of mounted birds, fish, and animals.

His decoys reflect his talent for relating the bird to its environment. The black duck decoy, illustrated here, is not the regular floating decoy. It is a "stick-up" and a "feeder," made to look like a duck eating. Under the bill is a steel clip that held fresh seaweed when the bird was staked out on the rocky shores of the St. Lawrence.

168. BLACK DUCK